The
Scott Fitzgerald Play

Michael McGuire

Copyright © 2015 by Michael McGuire

ISBN: 978-1-5040-2932-2

Distributed in 2016 by Open Road Distribution
180 Maiden Lane
New York, NY 10038
www.openroadmedia.com

For Galina

Do you see him? Do you see the story?
Do you see anything?

Heart of Darkness

Characters

Scott, 40

Zelda

Scottie, 9

Bunny

Monsignor

Ring

Edward

Doctor

Gerald

Sara

Act I

Darkness. Gradually the night view of the city reveals itself upstage. Faint traffic sounds. **SCOTT** *stands looking at the city. Smoke rises from the cigarette in his hand. His tortured bed is visible left. The light colored pajamas he wears are badly crumpled, his hair sticks to his scalp here and stands out from it there. Yet his movements are graceful.*

SCOTT (*Still looking at the city*): A prayer for those who cannot sleep.

SCOTT *crosses to the rickety table which can just be seen right, sits at the old Western Union typewriter, switches on the gooseneck lamp, puts out his cigarette. He begins to type with sudden speed.* **ZELDA** *appears behind him in crumpled hospital gown, barefoot, her hair cut short. Even when he answers,* **SCOTT** *neither sees nor hears her directly. Suddenly he stops typing, reads what he has written.*

SCOTT: Oh, God!
ZELDA: I know, Scott, I know.
SCOTT: This is terrible.

ZELDA (*Reading over his shoulder*): Yes. (*Softly.*) Scott, just sit here awhile. Let the people you know pass through your mind. If they have anything to say, they will say it. (*In his ear.*) It's '19. You're writing ads in New York. I'm in Montgomery, waiting for you. That's the feather fan you sent me in my hand.

> **SCOTT** *begins typing tentatively.*

ZELDA (*Reading*): No, Scott. You're not listening.

> **ZELDA**, *unseen by him, covers the typed page with her hand.* **SCOTT** *stops typing.*

ZELDA: Look! (**SCOTT** *looks into the distance.*) What do you see? (**SCOTT** *shrugs.*) See me dancing with an airman? (*He nods.*) How do you feel about it?
SCOTT: Awful.
ZELDA: What does he feel?
SCOTT: Nothing.
ZELDA: Perhaps. And me? What do I...?

> *Slight pause.*

SCOTT: I don't know.

> **ZELDA** *lifts her hand from the typewriter, takes a few thoughtful steps upstage, returns, stands somewhat behind* **SCOTT**.

ZELDA (*Referring to the image in his mind*): Look into my eyes, Scott. Listen to my voice.

SCOTT *begins typing slowly.*
ZELDA *reads over his shoulder.*

ZELDA: Yes, Scott. That's right. Feel the tightening in your brow? You're you, you're me, you're the airman. (*Taking leave of him.*) No selling, Scott. Never entertain.

> *As* **ZELDA** *disappears behind* **SCOTT***, his typing falters.* **BUNNY***, in suit and tie, appears standing left, surveying the room, the open bed and* **SCOTT** *coming to a stop. He is neither seen nor heard by* **SCOTT** *in this scene.*

BUNNY: Have you tried counting sheep? (*He approaches, stands beside* **SCOTT** *and pats the typewriter.*) I wouldn't worry about this. The work of our youth, well... We spend half our lives—depending on how long we live, of course—trying to suppress it. Steal a march on time, Scott. Throw it out now. (*Reading over* **SCOTT***'s shoulder.*) "We keep you clean in Muscatine." Well, it certainly has a ring to it. You have to survive, of course. There's no alternative. Not if you want the girl. That is what you want, isn't it: the girl? (**SCOTT** *nods slightly at his own thoughts.*) Then tie your muse down and take nickels at the door. This is America. (*Looking more closely at the page.*) I'd tighten my paragraphs, Scott, if I were you. Have you tried single-spacing? (*Beginning to leave, pausing.*) And oh, Scott: spelling.

> *Exit* **BUNNY** *behind* **SCOTT***.* **SCOTT** *places his hands on the typewriter a moment, then switches off the gooseneck light, crosses to the bed,*

and stands looking down at it.
ZELDA *appears near the night view
of the city, her gown alone making her
visible. She does not look at* **SCOTT**
in this scene.

ZELDA: If it's '31, Scott, you're out west, I'm alone in
Montgomery. But your hat's in the hall. I've left the light
on in your study. If I wake up at night, I can…
SCOTT (*Alone, interrupting, looking at bed*):
Princeton's losing. Third quarter, fourth down. "Who's
that young fellow over there throwing the ball? We
could use a new quarterback." "That's Scott Fitzgerald,
coach, hundred and thirty-five pounds, secretary of the
Triangle."
ZELDA: I'm studying your work now: every novel,
every story.
SCOTT (*Still looking at bed*): "Don't give me that crap!
I didn't ask his club. I don't care if he dresses up in
women's clothes. If he can throw the ball like that, we
want him in the game." (*Not to the physically present*
ZELDA.) I can't sleep, Zelda.

SCOTT *gets violently into bed, pulls
the covers up.*

ZELDA: Are you lying down? Are your eyes closed?
Tell me, Scott. It's so hard to keep it all straight. Is it the
beginning, or the end?
SCOTT (*Not to her*): It's the end, Zelda.
ZELDA: I'm always here, Scott. Always. Even then.
Are you asleep? (*Slight pause.*) Good, my friend. Sleep.
(*More softly.*) Scott Fitzgerald, you've been so good to
me.

ZELDA is gone. **SCOTT**, *eyes wide, counts in the darkness.*

SCOTT: Two stories at two hundred fifty each, three stories at seven hundred fifty each. Then, if I borrow five hundred...

> **SCOTT** *closes his eyes, exhales.* **BUNNY**, *wearing a conductor's cap, bends over him.*

BUNNY: Scott Fitzgerald...Scott Fitzgerald...

> *He switches on a light over* **SCOTT**'s *head.*

SCOTT (*"Waking" into his dream*): What...?
BUNNY: You told me to wake you up, sir. We're crossing the border now.
SCOTT (*Sitting up*): Crossing the..! What border?
BUNNY: We're on the bridge now, Mr. Fitzgerald. Hear it? If you look out, you can see way down.
SCOTT: I don't want to see way down. Wait a minute. Where's my...?
BUNNY: Your ticket? (*Producing it magically from inside* SCOTT's *pajamas.*) Here it is, sir. (*Unfolding it.*) Now let's see. Heading south, Mr. Fitzgerald?
SCOTT: Yes, conductor. I sold the novel. My girl...
BUNNY: Miss Zelda Sayre?
SCOTT: Why yes, conductor. How did you...?
BUNNY: This is the train for Paris.
SCOTT: Paris! Are you sure?
BUNNY: I work here, don't I? Where did you think you were going: Montgomery?
SCOTT: Why did you say Montgomery? Tell me that.
BUNNY: Why, it says Montgomery on your ticket, sir.

SCOTT (*Trying to get up*): Well, I'd better...
BUNNY (*Holding him in bed with one hand*): I'd forget it. It's easy to make a mistake in the station at night. All those trains. I sometimes get on the wrong one myself. Nothing to worry about. I do someone else's job. He does mine.
SCOTT: So what would you advise?
BUNNY: I'd go to sleep, sir, if I were you. I'd just catch a little shuteye.
SCOTT: You would? But...
BUNNY: But?
SCOTT: Where's my girl?
BUNNY: Your girl's down the line.
SCOTT: But...
BUNNY: But?
SCOTT: What if she's not there?
BUNNY: If she's not there, my friend, stay on the train. Somewhere between there and the next place just...
SCOTT: Just?
BUNNY: Step off into the night. It's that simple.
SCOTT: What if I just decide to get off your damn...
BUNNY (*Suddenly uncovering him*): Nothing simpler. This way to the observation platform, sir, and I'll...

> **BUNNY** *switches off light. Sounds of scuffle in the dark.* **ZELDA**, *as before plus red beret, stands in the light from a street lamp, right.* **SCOTT**, *in his pajamas, lies at her feet appallingly drunk, his speech slurred.*

ZELDA: What's wrong, honey? Got the bum's rush?
SCOTT: Must have. What's wrong with me?
ZELDA: Don't know, honey. No money? That's the usual.
SCOTT: Better give me the usual. Say, you're all right.

ZELDA: Am I?
SCOTT: I'll say. You know what I'd like?
ZELDA: Tell me.
SCOTT: I wonder if I might…
ZELDA: Sure. Why not? (*Bending closer.*) What is it, honey?
SCOTT: Can I just…

SCOTT *whispers in her ear.*

ZELDA (*Straightening, coldly*): You can't sleep here.
SCOTT: Why not? Where am I?
ZELDA: This place ain't got no name.
SCOTT: Don't tell me! It may not be Grand Central, but it's somewhere.
ZELDA: Yeah? Where?
SCOTT: Is it….Montgomery? My girl's in Montgomery.
ZELDA: Is she?
SCOTT: Yes. With a football player, with a pilot.
ZELDA: Make up your mind.
SCOTT (*Proudly*): With a…critic.
ZELDA: What's a critic?
SCOTT: A critic tells you when you're on the wrong train. He tells you where your girl is. He tells you what to do to get her back, and what to do if you can't.
ZELDA: They sound very useful.
SCOTT: The world could not get along without them.
ZELDA: How come I never met one?
SCOTT: They're not that plentiful. They don't go with girls like you.
ZELDA: They don't, huh? (*Looking around.*) You know, mister, I ain't had a nibble since you plopped yourself down. (*Leaving left.*) Think I'll just try another lamp post.
SCOTT: But what's your name?

ZELDA: No name.
SCOTT: But how will I…?
ZELDA (*Not looking back*): You won't.

> Exit **ZELDA** *as streetlights fades.*
> **SCOTT** *stands, realizes he is in his
> pajamas.*

SCOTT (*Not to the audience*): Ladies and gentlemen,
I… (*Slight pause.*) I wonder what time it is?

> *The bartender,* **BUNNY**, *appears
> behind his bar, right, polishing a glass
> and humming "It's three o'clock in the
> morning."*

SCOTT (*To himself*): I suppose I ought to…

> **BUNNY** *sets the glass on the bar.*

SCOTT (*In brogue*): "Have another, Mr. Fitzgerald."
(*Also in brogue.*) "Well, Mr. Fitzgerald, I believe I
will."

> **SCOTT**, *humming the second line of
> the song, dances briefly to the bar,
> exchanges manly smiles with the
> bartender, watches the glass filled, and
> looks down into it.*

SCOTT (*In brogue*): "And what's this, Bunny? Is it
meself upside down I see?" (*Raising his glass, looking
into it from the side. Straight.*) You know what I hold in
this glass, Bunny? Time. Yes, the hours, all the hours.
Including this one. Watch. You ought to appreciate this.
I'll make them vanish. One by one.

SCOTT *downs his drink, awaits another.* ZELDA *appears left, as before minus red beret, hot, tired, in her own world, looking down at her wristwatch.* SCOTT *does not look at* ZELDA *until indicated.* BUNNY *polishes glasses, not looking at* SCOTT *or* ZELDA, *but speaking so* SCOTT *alone can hear him.*

BUNNY: Mr. Fitzgerald, sir. It's your wife. (*No response*). Ask her if she's walked her five miles.
SCOTT (*Not looking*): Well, Zelda, have you walked your...
ZELDA (*To herself, interrupting, still looking at her watch*): I have a beautiful watch. My watch tells me it's eight-thirty.
SCOTT (*To himself, watching the empty glass on the bar*): I thought it was...
ZELDA (*To herself, interrupting*): I started at seven. Twenty minutes a mile. Half a mile to go.

She begins to leave, left.

BUNNY: She's leaving, Mr. Fitzgerald. Isn't there something you want to say to her?
SCOTT (*Raising his voice, but not looking*): Zelda... (*She stops, facing off.*) There's something I've been wanting to...
ZELDA (*Not turning, interrupting*): You should have thought of that at the party.
SCOTT: What party?
BUNNY (*For* SCOTT *alone*): ...the party's over...
SCOTT (*To* ZELDA, *without looking*): The party's over.

ZELDA (*Not looking, defiantly*): Is it?
SCOTT (*Beginning to face her*): Yes. It's time for my short peroration on...
BUNNY (*As before, his bartender's demeanor unchanged*): ...early death...
SCOTT (*Not so loudly*): Early death.
ZELDA: Good-bye, Scott.

> *Exit* **ZELDA**. **SCOTT**, *still facing downstage, has not looked at her.*

SCOTT (*Not looking at* **BUNNY**): You say that was my wife?
BUNNY: I believe so, Mr. Fitzgerald. Have another?

> **SCOTT** *hesitates, nods.* **BUNNY** *pours. At the sound,* **SCOTT** *turns to watch.*

SCOTT: There it is: a morning, an afternoon. And before you know it...

> **SCOTT** *raises his drink, sips.* **SCOTTIE,** *age 9, barefoot in nightgown, enters behind him, stops at some distance, looking down.*

BUNNY (*As before*): Mr. Fitzgerald, your daughter.
SCOTT (*Downing his drink, not turning*): What is it, Scottie? Why aren't you in bed?
SCOTTIE (*Still looking down*): Où est Maman?
SCOTT: Your mother's taking her walk, honey.
SCOTTIE (*Looking*): Mais, c'est trop tard! Elle va mieux, Papa?
SCOTT (*Not looking*): She seemed... I don't know. Go to bed, Scottie.

SCOTTIE: Papa. Qu'est ce qu'elle fait?
SCOTT: She's...
BUNNY (*As before*): ...writing a novel...
SCOTT: Your mother's writing a novel, Scottie.
SCOTTIE: Oh, Papa. Un roman! Are we in it?
SCOTT: I don't know, honey. I don't know.
BUNNY (*As before*): You don't know very much, do you?
SCOTTIE (*Immediately*): Are you taking me to the party, Papa?
SCOTT: What party?
SCOTTIE: Danse-tu avec moi?
SCOTT: I'll always...

> *As* **SCOTT** *turns toward her,*
> **SCOTTIE** *leaves the way she came.*

SCOTT (*Knowing she can't hear*): I'll always dance with you, Scottie.

> *Slight pause.*

BUNNY: Time for another, Mr. Fitzgerald?

> **SCOTT** *shrugs.* **BUNNY** *pours.*

SCOTT (*Watching*): An afternoon, an evening. What was that you said, Bunny?
BUNNY: Me, sir?
SCOTT: I thought you said something.

> **SCOTT** *sips his drink.* **ZELDA**
> *appears left wearing a luxurious*
> *ankle-length robe, though still*
> *barefoot. A Christmas tree is faintly*
> *visible behind her.* **SCOTTIE** *stands*

apart, facing downstage, looking down at the present in her hands.

ZELDA (*Softly*): Go on, dearest. Open it.
SCOTTIE: But who's it from?
SCOTT (*Not looking*): It's from your mother, Scottie.

SCOTTIE *happily tears it open, finding nothing as the box collapses in her hands.*

SCOTTIE (*Head down, not looking*): Maman, c'est vide.
ZELDA: You have to imagine, Scottie.
SCOTT (*Finishing his drink, not looking*): What should she imagine: that you love her?
BUNNY (*Polishing glasses, straight face, low voice*): That's the way, sir.
ZELDA: Why not? That's what I imagined when I wrapped it.
SCOTTIE: I don't understand.

SCOTTIE, *still facing downstage, moves center on her line. She is equidistant from her parents:* **SCOTT** *to her right,* **ZELDA** *to her left.*

SCOTT (*Turning towards her*): Of course you don't.
BUNNY: You tell them, Mr. Fitzgerald.
SCOTT (*Turning on him*): What did you say?
ZELDA (*Asking for help, softly*): Scott…
SCOTT (*Leaving his drink, taking a step towards* **SCOTTIE**): It's a magic present, Scottie. You look into the box and whatever you want will appear.
ZELDA: In a day or two.
SCOTTIE: In a day or…!

ZELDA (*Walking slowly towards* **SCOTTIE** *from the other side*): That is, if you can imagine… (*Stopping at a distance*). Are you imagining? You have to close your eyes. Doesn't she, Scott?

> *Slight pause.*

SCOTT: Of course.
SCOTTIE (*Eyes closed, reaching out a hand towards each of her parents*): I see…
ZELDA (*Interrupting, taking a step backwards*): If you tell, you won't get it. Ever.
SCOTT: Can't she just whisper it to her father?
ZELDA: There are rules. If you break one, you have to go back and start over.
SCOTTIE (*To* **ZELDA**, *not facing her*): Can I open my eyes now…?

> **ZELDA**, no longer hearing, turns to the Christmas tree.

SCOTTIE (*Barely audible*): … Mommy…?

> **ZELDA** *pops an ornament between her palms, and then another.* **SCOTT** *watches, horrified. Behind him* **BUNNY** *audibly fills his glass.* **SCOTTIE**, *sensing something is wrong, yet not wanting to see it, turns toward the sound of popping ornaments, her eyes still closed.*

SCOTTIE: Mom…

> *Another ornament pops.* **SCOTTIE** *turns away, opening her eyes, and runs*

off right without looking back.
ZELDA, *her hands still, looks at*
SCOTT.

ZELDA: Scott…

Slight pause. **SCOTT** *goes to her,
wipes her cut hands with his
handkerchief.*

ZELDA: We've gotten through this time, haven't we?
It's past, isn't it?
BUNNY: Your drink, Mr. Fitzgerald.
ZELDA: I didn't mean to. I don't want to. You know
that, don't you?
SCOTT (*Nodding, gently*): She knows too.
BUNNY: This one's on me, Mr. Fitzgerald.
ZELDA: Does she? (**SCOTT** *nods, turns from her.*) I
remember the pear trees.
SCOTT (*Hesitating*): Pear trees?
ZELDA: Outside my window.
SCOTT (*Moving towards bar*): Oh.
ZELDA (*In the voice of twenty years ago*): You're from
St. Paul, lieutenant? (**SCOTT** *stops, half turns toward
her.*) I never knew anyone from St. Paul.
SCOTT (*A young man's voice*): It's near Minneapolis.

*The light begins to change. Faint
sound of the dance, off; the scent of the
magnolias.*

ZELDA (*More unreservedly*): Oh, my!
SCOTT: Just the Mississippi between them.
ZELDA: The Mississippi… (*Approaching.*) Do boys
from Minneapolis get rich, lieutenant?
SCOTT: Some do.

ZELDA (*Hesitantly*): But not all? (*Moving away.*) How can you tell, lieutenant…which ones…? Is there something in the way they walk? (*Facing him.*) You were the best dancer there tonight. You're a gentleman, Scott Fitzgerald. Tell me about Princeton. I'm the daughter of a judge.

> *Changed light.* **BUNNY** *and the bar are gone. The porch swing has replaced the Christmas tree.*

ZELDA: Look! It's afternoon. You know me better now. You can sit on my porch.
SCOTT: Thank you.

> *They sit, swing leisurely.*

ZELDA: Tell me, Scott Fitzgerald: do you know what love is?
SCOTT: I think maybe I do.
ZELDA: But we were… What were we talking about? I want to be right there, you know.
SCOTT: Where?
ZELDA: In the middle. Where the chips are.
SCOTT: Is that what's in the middle?
ZELDA: Absolutely. The girl on green velvet, and the chips. But we were… What were we talking about?
SCOTT: Love.
ZELDA: Yes, love. Tell me about love, lieutenant.

> **SCOTT** *opens his mouth. There is the sound of a biplane diving low over the house.* **SCOTT** *stands angrily.*

ZELDA (*Calmly remaining seated*): Maybe you should ask him.

SCOTT: What?

ZELDA: Oh, I thought you knew.

SCOTT: You mean...

ZELDA: Yes. All the pilots. Every one of them. Can you tell me why I have so many admirers, lieutenant? Can you explain that?

> **SCOTT** *admits with a gesture that he cannot.*

ZELDA: Try.

> **SCOTT** *moves about lawyer-fashion.*

SCOTT: Did you run naked as a child?

ZELDA: Possibly.

SCOTT: Do you walk on airplane wings at state fairs?

ZELDA: Occasionally.

SCOTT (*Still*): And what do you do when...?

ZELDA: When...?

SCOTT: When you find yourself on the high board...

ZELDA: On the high board...

SCOTT: And you look down and there's no water in the...

ZELDA: ...no water...

> *The biplane dives again, seems about to crash, then pulls out of it. Neither* **SCOTT** *nor* **ZELDA** *has looked up. Slight pause.*

ZELDA: I think I say... (*From within*) ...Scott, Scott... (*Normally.*) Is that love?

SCOTT: I think so.

They look at each other. **SCOTT**
*returns to the swing. He is taking her
hands when* **BUNNY** *appears behind
them with two mint juleps on a tray.
He speaks in a minstrel's voice.*

BUNNY: "Miss Zelduh! Mr. Fitzgerald, suh!"
ZELDA: Mint juleps in my house! Does the judge
know?
BUNNY: "He ordered them specially, Miss Zelduh."
ZELDA (*Taking hers*): The judge's word is law.
SCOTT (*Taking his*): Thanks, Bunny.
BUNNY (Bowing and disappearing): "Suh!"

> **SCOTT** *and* **ZELDA** *raise their
> glasses to each other, nearly drink, but
> pause, speaking over their glasses.*

SCOTT: I see a time in which we will do something
other than what we ought to be doing.
ZELDA: What are you talking about?
SCOTT: And a time beyond time…
ZELDA (*Interrupting, lowering her drink*): What
nonsense!
SCOTT (*Lowering his drink*): …when it's used up,
gone.
ZELDA (*Standing, leaving her robe and drink on the
swing*): I don't like this kind of talk.

> **ZELDA** *moves away, then moves in
> another direction as the light begins to
> fade.*

ZELDA (*Stopping, anxious*): Scott?
SCOTT: What?
ZELDA: Is it night?

SCOTT (*Standing, leaving his drink on the swing*): It might be.

ZELDA *(Moving)*: ...Scott, Scott...

> **ZELDA** *moves in another direction as the light continues to fade. She stops, stays put until indicated.*

ZELDA (*Suddenly depressed, looking at the ground*): Where are we?

SCOTT: Verdun.

ZELDA: Oh, my God!

> *The swing is gone.* **BUNNY** *stands right, polishing.* **SCOTT***'s drink stands on the bar.*

ZELDA: Why did you bring me here?

SCOTT: It was a mistake.

ZELDA: I'm cold. Can we go back to the hotel?

SCOTT: They don't like us there.

ZELDA: Why not?

SCOTT: They think we're German.

ZELDA (*Not moving, laughing wildly*): "Ja, ich spreche so gut Deutsch!" (*Suddenly serious.*) Are we, Scott?

SCOTT: What?

ZELDA: German

SCOTT: We're all German, Zelda.

BUNNY (*Wiping the bar, low*): Speak for yourself, bud.

ZELDA (*Moving suddenly*): Ah! What's that? I think I've cut my ankle. (*Moving suddenly in another direction.*) Ah! There're more. What are they, Scott?

> **BUNNY** *holds up the Guide Michelin for* **SCOTT** *to see.* **SCOTT** *crosses.*

BUNNY *slides the Guide over the bar to him.*

SCOTT (*Reading*): "... la tranche des bayonets..."
ZELDA (*Afraid to move*): The...trench...of...
SCOTT (*Fingering his drink, not lifting it*): Of bayonets. Those are bayonets.
ZELDA: So? Why are they sticking up like that?
SCOTT: The men are underneath.
ZELDA: I don't believe it.
SCOTT: They crouched, waiting in the trench. A shell landed. (*Pointing to either side of* **ZELDA**.) There. Or there. The earth came silently. The darkness was solid. Their rifles wouldn't move.
ZELDA: It's late. It's going to rain. I felt a drop.
SCOTT (*Leaving his drink, approaching*): Go back to the car.

SCOTT *touches the ground.*

ZELDA: You'll ruin your suit.
SCOTT: Go.

SCOTT *crouches as* **ZELDA** *moves left.*

ZELDA (*Stopping*): Are you going to pray, Scott? I didn't know you prayed. It's not your noncombatant shell shock acting up again? (*Going "Southern," strutting along the line of unseen bayonets.*) Why, Scott Fitzgerald! I do believe you're jealous. What is it: their worn uniforms, the dirt in their eyes? Never to lift their heads, never to look up. We had set our sights a little higher, hadn't we? That's what they lie beneath, isn't it: the Twenties? (*Reciting.*) "Everyone clapped when we arose / For her pretty face and my new clothes."

SCOTT: Not here. You'll make the angel weep.
ZELDA: And why shouldn't they! (*Softly.*) We were obscene.
SCOTT (*Standing*): We were young.
ZELDA (*Realistically*): Now that we're not, do you think we might…

Slight pause.

SCOTT: Might what?
ZELDA (*Forcefully*): Might, just might!
SCOTT: It's an interesting suggestion, Zelda. A world of possibility there.

> *Exit* **ZELDA** *left as light fades on her side of the stage.* **BUNNY** *slides* **SCOTT**'s *drink toward him.*

BUNNY: You think you lost her that time, sir?
SCOTT (*Not touching his drink*): I might have.
BUNNY: Women are strange creatures.
SCOTT: They certainly are.
BUNNY: Just have to give them what they want.
SCOTT: Is that the secret?
BUNNY: That's it.
SCOTT (*Looking at his drink*): There it is: the light from the bathroom, the sound of the refrigerator…
BUNNY: What's that, sir?
SCOTT: The long night, Bunny. That's when our wives and children visit us. We put our arms around them.
BUNNY: Whatever you say, sir.
SCOTT (*Raising his drink*): Look.

> **SCOTT** *sips.* **ZELDA** *appears up left, still in her hospital gown, lowering a flown black "iron" fence in front of a*

small painted backdrop of trees, sky, birds in flight. The **DOCTOR** *is seated on the bench down left, a white jacket over her dress,* **ZELDA**'s *loose manuscript in her lap. Their conversation, as* **SCOTT**'s *and* **BUNNY**'s *is self-contained, though the scenes are indirectly aware of each other.*

ZELDA: Aren't you going to write any of this down?

DOCTOR (*Referring to the manuscript*): Aren't you the one who sees life as material?

ZELDA: It's nothing in itself.

DOCTOR: I don't believe that. Friends…

ZELDA (*Interrupting*): The only friend I ever had is over there bending his elbow.

———

BUNNY: How's that one, Mr. Fitzgerald?

SCOTT: I'm making it last, Bunny.

———

DOCTOR (*Laughing softly*): Do they always talk like that?

ZELDA: Just like that. (*Moving downstage.*) Tell me, doctor. Did you never meet that certain second lieutenant?

DOCTOR: I…

ZELDA (*Interrupting*): I see: you thought you had, but PERHAPS you hadn't. Now you wonder if, PERHAPS, after all, you might have.

DOCTOR (*Smiling*): You're right. You should be the…

ZELDA (*Interrupting*): Have you ever thought, PERHAPS, you're trying too hard? We don't all need stitches, Dr. Frankenstein.

DOCTOR: Dear Zelda, I know that.

_____

SCOTT: Did you ever hear the one about the lady doctor, Bunny?
BUNNY: No, sir. I don't believe I have.
SCOTT: Listen.

_____

DOCTOR (*Amused*): I don't believe *I've* heard the one about the lady doctor.
ZELDA: Neither have I. I'll get out of here.
DOCTOR: I never doubted it. I just want you to stay out once you're gone. We don't want you dying here.
ZELDA: Oh, I have no intention of that. But why shouldn't I?
DOCTOR: What? (*Slight pause.*) You asked me a question, Zelda.
ZELDA: Did I?
DOCTOR: You said "Why shouldn't I?" And I said "What?"
ZELDA: Why shouldn't I stay away?
DOCTOR (*Relieved*): Oh.
ZELDA: Why?
DOCTOR (*Fingering the pages of the manuscript*): I'm not sure you always know the difference between creating a character and being one.
ZELDA: Is there a difference?
DOCTOR: Oh, yes. One is all pretense.
ZELDA: Yes, but which one?

They laugh.

_____

SCOTT: Well? Well?

BUNNY (*Politely chuckling*): That's very funny, Mr. Fitzgerald. Only the way I heard it...
SCOTT (*Interrupting*): If you don't get it, you don't get it.

———

DOCTOR: We must have missed it.
ZELDA (*Ironically*): Damn! (*They giggle. Coldly.*) Well? (*The **DOCTOR** looks at her.*) I said "Which one?"
DOCTOR: I thought that was a joke.
ZELDA: It was. (*Rapidly.*) You said you weren't sure I know the difference between creating a character and being one, that was why you weren't sure I'd "stay away." I said "Is there a difference?" You said "Oh, yes one is all pretense. " I said "Which one?"
DOCTOR: I remember.
ZELDA: Well?
DOCTOR (*Warmly*): Well?
ZELDA: I asked you a question, doctor.

———

SCOTT (*Pushing his empty glass towards **BUNNY***): One more, Bunny,
BUNNY: Sorry, Mr. Fitzgerald. That's it.
SCOTT: What do you mean "That's it?"
BUNNY (*Taking away the bottle*): I mean that's it, sir. I'm sorry.
SCOTT (*Looking down into his empty glass*): But...
BUNNY (*Talking away the glass, his voice changed*): You think you'll find her there, you lush?
SCOTT: Who? What?
BUNNY (*His old self*): I beg your pardon.

> **SCOTT** *looks at him, then takes a few sudden steps downstage, stops. His*

light fades somewhat; **BUNNY** *and the bar are gone.*

_____

DOCTOR: You don't have to be "Zelda," Zelda. Don't worry about *who* you are. Just do.
ZELDA: What?
DOCTOR: What you do best.
ZELDA: And what's that?
DOCTOR (*Turning the pages of the manuscript*): I love your dancing scenes, and the ones with the child. By the end I want you to go on and on.

Slight pause.

ZELDA: Perhaps I will.
DOCTOR: I like your portrait too.
ZELDA: You do?

> **ZELDA** *moves a few steps downstage, stops.*

_____

SCOTT: Ladies and gentlemen, I…

> *He looks for his watch, finds he isn't wearing one, stands somewhat dazed.*

_____

DOCTOR (*Softly*): Zelda? (*Slight pause*). Zelda?
ZELDA (*Not looking, barely audible*): What?
DOCTOR: Zelda, I…

> *Realizing that* **ZELDA** *is no longer hearing, the* **DOCTOR** *stands, leaving*

the manuscript on the bench, and looks around her.

DOCTOR: I loved these trees, these birds. I wondered why people didn't just sit and look at them and stand up better.

*The **DOCTOR** goes to the black fence, raises it out of sight.*

ZELDA (*Not looking, not moving*): Why are you taking that away?
DOCTOR: There was a gate in it.

*The **DOCTOR** raises the painted backdrop.*

ZELDA (*Not looking*): What are you doing to the sky?
DOCTOR: Nothing, Zelda. The sky's all right.

*The **DOCTOR** smiles at **ZELDA**, leaves up left. **ZELDA** does not move as the light fades.*

ZELDA (*Barely audible*): …Scott, Scott…

SCOTT *becomes aware he is in his pajamas, looks around, spots his rumpled bed, crosses, lights a cigarette, stands looking out the window. It is quite dark now. **ZELDA** stands alone, not looking at **SCOTT**. The night view of the city is visible, as are **SCOTT***'s *profile and his cigarette. He does not look at **ZELDA** either, though they speak with the quiet* *intimacy of two people talking in an unlit room.*

ZELDA: Are you drinking?
SCOTT (*Looking out the window*): Not much. A little gin.
ZELDA: Are you sleeping?
SCOTT: I don't need much sleep, Zelda.
ZELDA: How's Scottie? What do you tell her? (**SCOTT** *inhales, releases his smoke.*) Scott, at night I stand at the window. I send whatever strength I have. To both of you. It leaves me, but it doesn't get beyond the grounds. Somewhere around the gate it falters. (*She laughs softly, sanely.*) If I could walk at night, it would stir about my ankles. Scott?
SCOTT: What?
ZELDA: How many novels have you written?
SCOTT: Oh, four, five, I...
ZELDA (*Interrupting*): And how many have I unwritten? I mean if it hadn't been for my "standard of living," my "entertainment," my doctor's bills, how many would you have...
SCOTT (*Interrupting, putting out his cigarette*): Four or five.
ZELDA: Do you mean that?

> **SCOTT** *nods, gets into his bed.*
> **ZELDA**, *for the first time, turns, picks up her manuscript, then approaches* **SCOTT** *silently, pauses, kisses his forehead, exits up left. A faint pre-dawn light behind the city.* **SCOTT** *sleeps.*

Act II

SCOTT's *bed is gone. The stage is opened up, spacious, no longer divided by lighting. The natural light of day now floods it from seaward, revealing* GERALD *in Twenties bathing costume, a beach umbrella under one arm, a couple of beach chairs under the other. Early morning. The day grows brighter as* GERALD *sets up.* SCOTT *lies curled in his pajamas down left. Just as the morning sun hits* SCOTT, GERALD *puts up the umbrella to shield him.*

GERALD (*Gazing off down left, seaward*): It's almost worth it.

SCOTT, *otherwise motionless, opens his eyes.*

GERALD: I mean this light. It's almost worth last night's...dark. Where did we end up last night? I remember. You certainly made a fool of yourself, Scott. I tried to make amends. I gave the old woman something.

SCOTT *remembers.*

GERALD (*Sitting in one of the chairs*): Forget it. You've done worse. (*Shaking out his Herald Tribune.*) We all have. (*Reading.*) "Businessman jumps from tall building." What does he know that I don't? (*Looking around*.) What do you think, Scott? I think the beach is the nearest we ever come to...is perhaps all we ever know of... Oh, I know what you'll say: what about the party? Frankly, Scott, just the thought of planning an evening to contradict what the light of day has shown us so plainly to be true...

> **ZELDA** *appears up right in Twenties bathing costume, motionless, listening. She does not move until indicated. She speaks when she senses the others have become aware of her.* **SCOTT**, *not looking when she speaks, remains curled on his side, facing downstage. The sun grows steadily brighter.*

ZELDA: Do you dye the water, Gerald?
GERALD: Of course. (*Looking out to sea*.) Today's color is...
ZELDA: Milk white, with a touch of green. I didn't know you let it get so hot on your beach, Gerald.
GERALD: I usually don't.
ZELDA: Do you allow bums on your beach, Gerald?
GERALD: To whom are you referring?
ZELDA: The object at the water's edge.
GERALD: Shh. That's our writer-in-residence. He's catching forty winks. He wrote all night.
ZELDA: And the old woman, what did she do?
GERALD (*Offering a chair*): Welcome to our deliberations, Zelda.

> **ZELDA** *approaches, sits.*

SCOTT: Sometime, Gerald, I wonder if you ever knew what you were capable of.
ZELDA (*To* **GERALD**): What's he talking about?

GERALD (*To* **ZELDA**): I'm not sure.

SCOTT (*Raising himself on one elbow, still looking seaward*): Gerald, you held them in the palm of your hand. You lifted them up.

GERALD: Who?

ZELDA: What?

GERALD (*Assuming he understands, to* **SCOTT**): The poor are always with us.

SCOTT: So is life untouched by any grace. In my dreams, I swim. I can't get my arms and legs to work together. I can't seem… to turn my head…to breathe. The sea is full.

ZELDA (*Very softly*): Of what?

SCOTT: People.

> **SCOTT** *turns his head slowly, looks intensely at* **GERALD**.

ZELDA (*Looking away*): Do you ever get the feeling you're being observed, Gerald.

GERALD: I do at times.

SCOTT (*Looking front*): You invite them over, you fill their glasses…

GERALD: Why? Who? Not the poor.

SCOTT (*As before*): You make up the guest list, Gerald. It's one of your arts.

GERALD: I'm sorry, Scott. I'm lost.

SCOTT (*Looking out to sea*): And I thought you, if anyone, understood the hopeless gesture, the attempt when failure is certain.

ZELDA (*To* **GERALD**): How does it feel to be Scott's study in…. In what?

GERALD (*Shrugging*): Hopeless gestures?

ZELDA: He's going to put you in a book, Gerald. How do you feel about that? Isn't there something you want to hold onto?

GERALD: What? (*Looking around him.*) This light?

SCOTT: It's a mistake.

GERALD: What is?

SCOTT: To think we live. We lay out the blank paper. The days pass. We stand up weaker than we sat down.

GERALD (*To* **ZELDA**): He's off again.

ZELDA (*To* **GERALD**): I don't understand a word of it, do you?

SCOTT: We reach behind us. We can't reach far. We only reach a few. What presumption! There's nothing in these hands. We reach in front of us. I want to say "Dear Reader," but the time's not right.

> **GERALD** *goes to the umbrella, adjusts it to shade* **SCOTT***, returns to his chair.*

ZELDA: What about you, Gerald? Is it getting any easier?

GERALD: I was never at ease in this life. Perhaps I've made it easier for others.

ZELDA (*Amused*): I see. The perfects host was not at home. He only pretended to be. We, the perfect guests, pretended to arrive.

GERALD (*Looking from* **ZELDA** *to* **SCOTT** *to* **ZELDA**): I'm sure I saw you both at one of our little get-togethers. Wasn't that you?

ZELDA: It was me all right, Gerald. Though I may have been alone. After all, a clean collar, an interesting tie, and there you have him.

GERALD: Who?

ZELDA: Man. Papier-mâché man. The anthropologists…

> *Slight pause.*

GERALD: What about the anthropologists?

> **ZELDA**, *unable to talk any longer, covers her eyes.* **SCOTT**, *aware of her but not looking at her, stands.*

SCOTT: Inferno, Gerald, is this damn light on our lives. Purgatory was the first crack between earth and sky. Perhaps it's when we dance the whole night through. That's all we'll ever know of...

GERALD: Of what?

> **SCOTT** *spreads his arms expansively;* **GERALD** *looks around him.*

GERALD: Ah! I understand. You're talking about the party, in the abstract. The idea of the party. Nights that redeem our days. A guest list of the damned. Am I right? That's the hopeless gesture, isn't it: our little celebration?

SCOTT (*Removing his pajama top, going towards the water down left*) I wonder: does papier-mâché melt?

ZELDA (*Her eyes still covered, very softly to* **SCOTT**, *concerned*): Don't.

SCOTT (*Stopping, not looking at her*): Don't what?

ZELDA (*Uncovering her eyes, attempting to speak normally to* **GERALD**): I think Scott should save himself for tonight, don't you?

GERALD: What does he have to do tonight?

ZELDA: Pretend to arrive, pretend to be there. And escort me.

GERALD (*Standing*): That, I'm sure, is what he most looks forward to.

ZELDA: Oh, Gerald.

GERALD: And should his arm in any way prove inadequate, you always have mine.

SCOTT: Good. That's settled. (*Looking seaward.*) I'll swim out to the raft now, and under it.

ZELDA (*Standing, softly*): I love to swim under things.

SCOTT: Popping up the other side, I'll splash on to…to Corsica.

GERALD: I hope you can get your arms and legs to work together.

SCOTT (*Moving towards the water*): I'll try.

ZELDA: I'm thinking about the children.

SCOTT (*Stopping, still looking seaward*): What children?

ZELDA (*Approaching behind him*): Dick's and Nicole's. Do you think, in later years, they ever came looking for their father?

SCOTT (*Facing her*): Why not? They could ask at all the grocery stores.

ZELDA: They could drag the lakes.

> **SCOTT** *and* **ZELDA** *chuckle.* **GERALD** *sits, returns to his paper.*

SCOTT: Can I sleep now, Zelda?

ZELDA: Yes, my dearest. Put your head down. The sand's warm, it fits your body. I'll sit here beside you. I'll listen to your stories. You end them, but I know they go on.

SCOTT: Swim, Zelda. Go on. I'll watch.

> **ZELDA** *hesitates, exits towards the water.* **SCOTT** *watches a moment, returns to the shade of the umbrella, sits, watches, then lies on his back and closes his eyes.*

GERALD (*Behind his paper*): "Author Drowns Trying to Save Reputation."

SCOTT, *eyes closed, arms and legs spread, does not respond. Slight pause. Enter* BUNNY, *the lifeguard, right, on duty, "PARADISE" lettered across the chest of his bathing costume. He stands over* SCOTT, *speaks softly.*

BUNNY: Feel it, Scott? The curve of the earth! Where are you, old man? Rockville Union Cemetery, Zelda at your side and your father across the road? Listen to the rain, Scott. The paths must be slick, treacherous.

SCOTT*'s eyes open, meet* BUNNY*'s.*

BUNNY (*Normally*): You can't sleep here, fella.
SCOTT: Why not?
BUNNY: Private property.

BUNNY, *having warned* SCOTT, *exits left, along the beach.* GERALD *chuckles.*

GERALD (*Behind his paper*): You know what's happening to the dollar, Scott? You want to hear the price of gold?

ZELDA *calls incomprehensibly from the water, then laughs. Both men look.*

GERALD: What did she say?
SCOTT: Couldn't hear.

SCOTT *sits up. They watch her swim.*

GERALD: There's grace.
SCOTT: I never denied it.

GERALD: I thought you said she was afraid.
SCOTT: Zelda? Never. (*Slight pause*). I used to think if I got the girl, the rest would follow.
GERALD: And so it has.
SCOTT (*Smiling*): You mean this is it.
GERALD: This is always it.

> *Enter* **ZELDA** *left in wet bathing suit.*

GERALD (*To* **ZELDA**): What did you say?
ZELDA (*Taking off her cap, shaking her head*): Say?
SCOTT: We heard you calling.
ZELDA: Not me.
SCOTT: There's no one else out there.

> *All look out to sea.*

ZELDA (*Very softly*): Scott…

> **SCOTT** *and* **ZELDA** *look at each other, both frightened.*

GERALD (*Standing*): Time to set up.
ZELDA (*Normally*): Oh?
GERALD: Our guests will be arriving. Our second string, of course.
ZELDA: Of course.

> *Exit* **GERALD** *right.* **ZELDA** *towels herself while* **SCOTT** *watches.*

SCOTT: Perhaps you'd like to know why I'm sitting here on the porch in St. Paul.
ZELDA: If you'd like to tell me.
SCOTT: Because I've written all morning.
ZELDA: Good, Scott. I'm glad.

SCOTT: I'm just listening to the day move on without me now. In a moment I'm going for my walk. Then it will be time for my nap.

ZELDA (*Approaching*): How old are you, Scott?

SCOTT: Forty-five, or six.

ZELDA (*Sitting by him*): Oh, Scott.

> **SCOTT** *lies back, closes his eyes. The sky darkens, the surf becomes audible, a cool wind stirs the umbrella, the chairs.* **ZELDA** *shivers.*

SCOTT (*Eyes still closed*): I thought we were on Cap d'Antibes.

ZELDA (*Covering* **SCOTT** *with his pajama top*): No. This is the wind off Lake Superior; these are the leaves of Summit Avenue blowing around us.

SCOTT: Oaks, elms.

ZELDA: Maples.

SCOTT: Is this the country where the best run after the worst?

ZELDA: This is it.

SCOTT: I thought it might be.

ZELDA: Scott… It's France,1929.

SCOTT: Is it?

ZELDA: Or' 31 or '35. You didn't write this morning.

SCOTT (*Opening eyes*): I didn't?

> *The wind drops as* **GERALD** *and* **SARA** *enter right in evening clothes. They stand close together, far from* **SCOTT** *and* **ZELDA**.

SARA: What happened to the day? The sun just came up. Is it getting dark, Gerald?

GERALD (*Setting up for cocktails*): Seems to be, Sara.

SARA: But why?

GERALD: I felt we needed a little change in the lighting. Our guests did.

_____

ZELDA (*Leaning closer to* **SCOTT**): What about your nap?

SCOTT: Nap?

ZELDA: You went for your walk, you kicked the leaves. The neighbors said "Who is that old guy kicking the leaves?" It was time for your nap.

SCOTT: I must have missed it.

_____

> **GERALD** *pours.*

SARA (*To* **GERALD**): A Dubonnet for Zelda.

GERALD (*To himself*): A gin and tonic for our author.

_____

ZELDA (*Still seated next to* **SCOTT***, her voice soft*): Are you dreaming, Scott? A warm sea holds you up, you're flying close to the sun, you're diving. No. No, it isn't you. It's me.

> **ZELDA** *laughs briefly, harshly, starts left.* **SCOTT** *stiffens.*

SARA (*Quietly*): Gerald, the rocks.

GERALD (*Raising his voice*): Not in the dark, Zelda. I wouldn't.

ZELDA: I'm sure you wouldn't.

> *Exit* **ZELDA.**

SARA: Scott, do something!

SCOTT (*Refusing to move*): She's not a character in a book.

GERALD: But does she know it?

> **GERALD** *and* **SARA** *look up to where* **ZELDA** *pauses on the rocks.*

SARA (*Softly*): Zelda, don't.

ZELDA (*Off*): Dark night, ancient sea, receive…

> *Her voice trails off.*

SCOTT (*Soft, almost a prayer*): Receive this dancer's body.

> **GERALD** *and* **SARA** *watch* **ZELDA** *dive.* **SCOTT** *stands, exits slowly left, pulling on his pajama tops.*

SARA: Where is she? Is she all night? There she is!

GERALD: I wouldn't do it, Scott.

> **GERALD** *and* **SARA** *watch* **SCOTT** *climb the rocks off. Enter* **ZELDA**, *wet.*

ZELDA: Well, where is he?

> **ZELDA**, *understanding, turns her back to the rocks. Enter* **SCOTT** *left, behind her, still in dry pajamas.*

GERALD: There he is.

ZELDA (*Not looking*): Paddling around?

GERALD: You might say that.

SCOTT: You know what happened, Gerald? Suddenly I was so…

SCOTT *yawns.* **ZELDA**, *not looking, laughs.*

SARA: You were wise, Scott.

> **GERALD** *picks up his guests' drinks to offer them.* **ZELDA** *starts left.*

SARA: Where are you going?
ZELDA: Anybody can do anything once.

> *Exit* **ZELDA**. **GERALD** *sets down the drinks. All watch.*

GERALD (*To* **SCOTT**): That's higher than you went, my friend.
SCOTT (*Calling*): Zelda…!
ZELDA (*Off*): What…?
SCOTT: You can't see in the dark!
ZELDA (*Off*): No…! Only writers can …!
SARA: She's at the top.
ZELDA (*Off*): I'm at the top. Goofo!
SARA: Don't let her do it, Scott.

> **SCOTT** *turns his back to the rocks.*

GERALD: Don't do it, Zel…!

> **GERALD** *and* **SARA** *watch as* **ZELDA** *dives, then search the dark water.*

SARA: Is that her?
GERALD: Where?

ZELDA (*Calling from the water*): Scott Fitzgerald, Scott Fitzgerald…!

Exit **SCOTT** *left.*

GERALD: Don't be a fool.
SARA: Scott, don't!
GERALD: My God, he's running up.

> **ZELDA** *laughs, stays in the water.* **GERALD** *and* **SARA**, *silent, watch* **SCOTT** *dive.*

SARA: There he is.
GERALD (*Calling*): Are you all right…?
SARA: He's swimming.
GERALD: She's swimming away.
SARA: He's following.

> **ZELDA** *is heard again, her laugh fading. Slight pause.* **GERALD** *and* **SARA** *speak more softly.*

GERALD: Birds.
SARA: Fish.
GERALD: It was all a game.
SARA: They're gone. (*Picking up* **ZELDA**'s *Dubonnet.*) Do you think Zelda would mind?
GERALD (*Picking up SCOTT's gin and tonic*): Do you think Scott would?

They raise their glasses.

SARA: To sleep.
GERALD: Sleep? To our wives, rescued.
SARA: To deep sleep.

GERALD: To Scott and Zelda. (*Raising his glass higher.*) Prayers.

SARA (*Raising hers*): Prayers.

> As **GERALD** *and* **SARA** *sip their drinks, the string of colored lights comes on.* **BUNNY**, *also formally attired, standing behind a card table, shuffles the cards once spectacularly in midair, smiles at* **GERALD** *and* **SARA**.

SARA (*Softly*): Shall we join the party?

GERALD (*Softly*): Might as well. It's ours. (*Normally, as they approach.*) Up to your old tricks, Bunny?

BUNNY: Take a card, Sara, any one.

SARA: Why thank you, Bunny. I choose…this one.

BUNNY: Take a look at it. Don't let me see. Now put it back.

> *She does so. Spectacular shuffle. The deck held out to* **GERALD**.

BUNNY: Take a card, Gerald, any one.

> **GERALD** *does so, returns it to the pack. Spectacular shuffle.* **BUNNY** *snaps out a card, presents it to* **SARA**.

BUNNY: Is this your card, Sara?

SARA: Why, Bunny! How do you do it?

BUNNY (*Not looking at the card*): The queen of diamonds. Notice the drop of water on your card, Sara. Just the splash one of our guests made that summer she dove from the rocks.

GERALD: What about my card, Bunny?

BUNNY (*Snapping one out*): Is this it?

GERALD: How…?
BUNNY (*Not looking*): The king of hearts. (*Holding it up.*) See the drop of blood, Gerald?
SARA: Bunny!
BUNNY: Of wine, Sara, of wine. Or is it ink? A drop dropped from the still pen of our short-lived resi… (*Suddenly lowering his head, his voice priestlike, low.*) Now let us…
SARA: Now let us what? For whom?

> *Enter* **SCOTT** *and* **ZELDA** *from seaward, down left, behind* **SARA** *and* **GERALD**. **ZELDA** *wears an evening dress,* **SCOTT** *a dinner jacket and striped pants. His pajamas protrude several inches at sleeve and cuff.*

BUNNY (*Normally*): I believe your guests have arrived.
GERALD (*Turning*): If it isn't the beautiful Zelda Fitzgerald!
ZELDA: And the gracious Gerald Murphy.

> *All move about.*

GERALD: Hello, Scott. Alive and kicking?
SARA: Why shouldn't he be?
SCOTT: Sara. Gerald. You may listen to my heart anytime.
BUNNY (*Low, to* **GERALD**): I'd hurry up if I were you.
SARA (*A quiet warning*): Bunny.
SCOTT: It is tonight, isn't it?
GERALD: What's that?
SCOTT: You were going to give a truly bad party. I thought that's why we were invited.

> **GERALD** *and* **SARA** *laugh.*

ZELDA: Don't let us down, Gerald. Scott is prepared to throw your best glasses over the cliff. I'm going to throw myself, but not until I lift my skirt to dance for you.

SARA: Well, if it makes you happy, my dears, of course. We never stop loving you.

SCOTT: But first I'm going to sing a song about a dog.

BUNNY (*Trying to lead* **SCOTT** *aside*): As your editor, Scott, I'd like to suggest a few revisions...

SCOTT (*Freeing himself*): Ladies and gentlemen, "The Song of the Dog."

> *Scattered polite applause during which* **BUNNY** *exits right. Slight pause.*

SCOTT: I seem to have...That is, I don't...

> **BUNNY** *reappears at his side bearing a full tray of champagne glasses.*

BUNNY (*Whispering to* **SCOTT**): Pol Roger Brut, monsieur. '19.

SCOTT (*Loudly*): Come on, someone. All I need is a little hint. What do dogs do?

ZELDA: Come on, everyone! What kind of a party is this?

GERALD (*An unsuccessful effort at letting go*): A bad one!

SARA (*Ditto*): Yahoo!

> *An effort is made.* **SARA** *drains her glass.* **ZELDA** *slips out of her black lace panties, tosses them to* **GERALD**.

GERALD: What do I do with these?

But **SCOTT** *outdoes them all, groveling on all fours, lifting his leg dog-fashion against* **GERALD**'s *pants leg, snuffling at* **SARA**'s *crotch.* **BUNNY**, *free of the tray, once more the editor, bends to speak to* **SCOTT**.

BUNNY (*To him alone*): It won't work, Scott. Parties are out.
SCOTT: What's in?
BUNNY: Have you thought of making Dick a coal miner? Nicole could sell apples. They meet in a soup kitchen.
SCOTT: Where do they go from there?
BUNNY: Down.
SCOTT (*Arms suddenly raised, tentatively barking*): Bruff? Bruff?

Suddenly **SCOTT** *yawns, begins to sag over.* **GERALD** *and* **BUNNY** *immediately hoist him to his feet.* **ZELDA** *places a glass in his hand.* **SARA** *kisses him on the cheek.* **SCOTT** *begins talking immediately.*

SCOTT: Let me tell you how it happened. I held that lovely glass in my hand. I said: this is living: there'll never be a fuller, happier moment.
GERALD: Then why not set the glass down, full, intact?
BUNNY: For another man to drink?
ZELDA: Scott wants to drain the glass, then eat it.
BUNNY: A slight overstatement.
SARA: I love overstatement.
SCOTT: We couldn't believe we held it…in our hands. (*Raising his glass somewhat, holding it there until indicated.*) We had to reach a little further….
ZELDA: Reach for it, hell. We chased it.

GERALD: But the Fitzgeralds chasing were not such an unlovely picture.

BUNNY: Nor, on the other hand, what I would call a masterpiece.

SARA: I agree with Gerald, of course.

ZELDA: of course.

Slight pause.

ZELDA: ladies and gentlemen, the great Scott Fitzgerald is silent. The song of the dog is sung. Now before I dance…

BUNNY: Before you throw yourself over the cliff.

ZELDA: Yes. Thank you, Bunny. Before I…

> *The **DOCTOR** enters right, her white jacket over her shoulders holding the hem of her evening dress above the sand.*

ZELDA: You here?

DOCTOR: Why not? How are you, Zelda?

ZELDA: I'm fine. Where was I?

BUNNY: La Cote d'Azur, 1924, 1929, 1931…

SARA: With your friends.

ZELDA: Yes. Well, before I…as I said…

> *Slight pause. **SCOTT** throws his glass off right. It breaks. **SARA**, graciously, throws hers. It, too, is heard breaking.*

ZELDA: I…

GERALD (*Helpfully*): Yes, Zelda?

ZELDA: Since the life Scott wrote was mine, I wondered, legitimately, how he had turned life into art. I read every novel, every story. I found myself loving him again.

DOCTOR: I think I understand.

SARA: I do too.
ZELDA (*To* SCOTT): I could never write like you. That's
what I should have done, Scott: painted. But my eyes…
SCOTT (*Softly*): Dance for us, Zelda.
ZELDA (*Drawn towards the sea*): The sea is black.
GERALD: We formally request you, Zelda, on behalf of
the night sky, the sea…
ZELDA: The sea. Very well.

> ZELDA *raises her evening gown to
> dance.* BUNNY, *once more bearing a
> tray of full glasses, appears at her side.*

BUNNY (*For her alone*): Il ne faut pas. Madame is too
old.
ZELDA (*Uncertainly*): What shall I…?
BUNNY: Pray.

> BUNNY *moves on to the other guests.*
> SCOTTIE, *nine, appears left, watching.*
> ZELDA, *tentatively, begins a Duncan-
> type dance, falls suddenly to her knees,
> head bowed.*

BUNNY (*Almost an aside*): Brought her down in one.
What scribbler can claim as much?
SARA: Thank you, Zelda.
DOCTOR: Thank you for dancing for us.
GERALD: Yes. That is what we mean to say.

> ZELDA *begins to gather small invisible
> objects with one hand, cradling them in
> the other.*

ZELDA: …old woman, old woman…we're so sorry…

SARA *and the* DOCTOR *go to* ZELDA, *raise her to her feet.* SCOTT, *having drained another glass, suddenly smashes it.*

GERALD: Scott, I must ask you to refrain. Those are our best...

ZELDA *suddenly rushes off right.* GERALD *and* SARA *freeze.* SCOTTIE *covers her eyes.*

The DOCTOR *watches.*

At the moment at which a falling ZELDA *would hit the ground,* SCOTT *breaks another glass.* BUNNY, *behind the table, gives one spectacular shuffle of his cards.* SCOTT *sits in one of the beach chairs. A brief gust of wind causes the colored lights to dance.* SARA *exits right, returns almost immediately with the stained handkerchief she has picked up.* GERALD *and the* DOCTOR *have not moved.*

GERALD: Well?
SARA: Not there.
DOCTOR: What's that?
SARA: Nothing. Blood from her knees.
GERALD: Picked herself up, I guess. Went home. I'd better tell Scott.

SARA *nods.* GERALD *crosses to* SCOTT, *bends over him, steps back.*

The **DOCTOR** *goes to one side of*
SCOTT, SARA *to the other.*

SARA: What is it?
GERALD (*Moving away, softly*): Nothing. He's asleep.
DOCTOR: Sleep, Scott Fitzgerald.
SARA: Sleep.

BUNNY, *ignoring the others, silently deals his cards.* **GERALD, SARA,** *and the* **DOCTOR** *wander separately off right.* **BUNNY,** *his cards dealt, follows the others.* **SCOTTIE** *uncovers her eyes. Another brief gust scatters the cards.* **SCOTT** *opens his eyes, perceives himself alone, stands, crosses down right, lights a cigarette, then crosses up left. As the beach fades behind him, the lights of the city appear before him.* **SCOTTIE,** *unseen by him, watches. The sky over the city lightens.* **SCOTT** *is visible only in silhouette as he draws once more on his cigarette, exhales.*

SCOTT: First light. Party over. Prayer said.

Light fades.

Act III

> ZELDA, *short hair, hospital gown and robe, a pair of embroidered slippers in her hands, stands downstage, left of center, stationary. The* DOCTOR, *in her usual white jacket, stands up left by the backdrop of painted trees and birds, the iron fence. She does not move. Summer afternoon light. Stage right in shadow.* ZELDA, *unaware of the* DOCTOR, *speaks indirectly to the spot where she imagines her mother to stand.*

ZELDA: Doctor says I've made such progress. I walk about now, as you see, unattended. Sometimes I take the bus into town. I take someone along, some one more disturbed than I.

(*Of the slippers.*) They're lovely, really. I hope they fit.

I've been thinking of the summer Scott proposed. Was it '19, mother? Or was I nineteen? It was hot.

I said "no." My tongue touched the roof of my mouth. And again "no." He seemed to accept it then. He left. He took the train to St. Paul. He sat in his room. He made it right. Max thought so. Scott wanted it published right away. It wasn't the fame. It was me.

…this…side…of…

> *She laughs briefly, looks around her, looks down.*

ZELDA: That was my novel, that one and the next. And the next. But not the last. No. (*Looking down at the*

slippers.) Though maybe alone in his room at the end...he would have called on me. What do you think? (*Suddenly radiant.*) He wired: Darling girl, or something like that, novel accepted, can I come? Of course, I said, or something like that, everything's changed. Come.
It was September. He was sure of himself again, the way he had been in his uniform. I watched him through the curtains...

> *She lowers her head. Slight pause.*

DOCTOR (*Stationary; gently*): You were nineteen.
ZELDA (*Delighted*): Was I? Nineteen!

> *For the first time* **ZELDA** *speaks directly to the spot where she imagines her mother to stand.*

ZELDA (*Changed*): What was it like, mother, after I left? Was there...something you had to say to each other, something you couldn't say while I...? Was there anything when I was five or six or nine to ever make you think you'd...

> *At the moment* **ZELDA**'s *eyes take in the grounds in a sweeping glance, she imagines* **SCOTT** *to appear.*

ZELDA (*Manic*): Why, isn't that Scott Fitzgerald? Scott Fitzgerald the writer!

> **ZELDA**, *moving for the first time in this scene, suddenly positions herself, with some flare, between "Scott" and her "mother." The* **DOCTOR** *doesn't move.*

ZELDA: This is my mother, Scott. This is Scott, mother. Oh I know he looks a little, well, ravaged, but I wanted you to see him as he would be, later. Scott, aren't you going to say something? Mother? (*Slight pause. Indirectly, to the* **DOCTOR**.) Aren't these the visiting hours?

> The **DOCTOR**, *unseen by* **ZELDA**, *looks at her watch, nods.* **ZELDA** *remains motionless, not in direct communication with the scene right, where the light now rises on* **SCOTT**, *in Hollywood suit and tie, seated in one of two identical chairs at a child-size desk which bears a toy typewriter and a toy telephone into which* **SCOTT** *is speaking.*

SCOTT: Of course not, Bernie, a tear-jerker never killed anyone. It's just that I... Listen, Bernie. Have I got one for you! Soft focus. (*Sotto voce.*) You'll have your hands in their pockets. (*Normally.*) I said they'll have their hearts in their mouths. What, Bernie? A conference? Now? I usually get a call from my little girl. I'm worried about her. She's at school and...

> **SCOTT** *looks at the dead receiver in his hand.* **ZELDA** *speaks front.*

ZELDA: It's me. Scott. You told me to call if they weren't helping. I...

> **ZELDA** *stops suddenly as* **SCOTT** *replaces the dead receiver.* **SCOTT** *stands, takes a few steps, speaks right*

as if he is just looking into another office.

SCOTT (*Tough*): Hey, kid. Listen to this one. Man owns a pool. Perfect host. Makes his guests happy. Bad times. Loses all. Shows up one day as lifeguard. At his own pool. Big party. No one knows him. So he thinks. What do you think? Will they laugh? Not the people around the pool! Goes without saying: they're in hysterics. I mean the great American Public. (*Slight pause.*) Well, just thought I'd ask. You won't steal it from me now?

> **SCOTT** *returns to his desk, sits with his hands on the typewriter, which is so small his hands cover it.*

ZELDA (*Looking down, softly*): Remember, Scott, our first crossing, our first storm? There's a story there.

> *Suddenly* **SCOTT** *is speaking on the telephone.*

SCOTT: Hi, Scottie! My love... You're not Scottie. You're her roommate. I knew it. The voice. You're her new roommate? She can't get along with anyone? You're there against your will? Listen, this is long distance. Could you please bring Scottie to the phone? She's learning how to pick up the right fork? Very interesting. And very important. I'm sure a call from her father at such a moment could only be...

> *Again* **SCOTT** *is looking at the dead receiver in his hand.*

ZELDA: Then there was Cherbourg, the French coast...

SCOTT *replaces the receiver, keeping his hand on it.*

SCOTT *(Softly):* I only wanted to tell you, Scottie, about those people who send their children to private schools.

SCOTT *suddenly lifts the receiver, about to dial.*

ZELDA: So much motion, Scott. What did it all mean?

SCOTT *hangs up, looks at his watch, places his fingers on the typewriter keys as the **DOCTOR**, looking at her watch, moves for the first time, towards **ZELDA**, but stopping short.*

DOCTOR: I know, Zelda, how people seem to be there...
SCOTT *(To himself)*: ... nothing...
ZELDA *(Looking down, softly)*: Paris, Scott.
DOCTOR: I beg your pardon.
ZELDA *(Softly)*: There was a novel in Paris, Scott. Is there a novel there too?

*The **DOCTOR** approaches **ZELDA**, bends closer, listens. **SCOTT** begins typing slowly, one word, then another.*

DOCTOR *(Gently)*: There's no one, Zelda.
ZELDA *(Softly)*: There's you.
DOCTOR: There's me.
ZELDA *(Indirectly to the **DOCTOR**, but of **SCOTT**)*: It's all right if there's a novel there too.
DOCTOR: That's good.

The toy phone rings for the first time.
SCOTT *answers.*

SCOTT: What's that, Bernie? Do I know what time it is? Haven't you got a watch? (*Sotto voce*) All right, Bernie, I'll tie her to the tracks. (*Normally.*) I said I'll fill in all the cracks. I'll... (*Ripping the phone cord out.*) Sorry, Bernie. We were disconnected.

> **SCOTT** *hangs up the dead receiver, returns his hands to the typewriter, but does not type.*

DOCTOR: As long as we don't talk to them, Zelda, no one knows...
ZELDA: No one knows what?
DOCTOR: No one knows we think we're not alone.

> *Slight pause.*

ZELDA: Is it time?
DOCTOR: Almost.
ZELDA: I'd like to stay here by myself a moment, if it's all right.

> *The* **DOCTOR** *nods, leaves slowly up left. The sun begins to lose its brightness.* **ZELDA** *speaks front.*

ZELDA: I'm going to bed now, Scott. I'm in a different time zone, you know. Oh, I know where I am, Scott. I'm so sorry for them, so sorry.

> **ZELDA** *doesn't move.* **SCOTT** *picks up the disconnected receiver.*

SCOTT: Zelda? Listen, Zelda. I'll make you a deal: you get me out of here. I'll get you out of there. What? As long as I get you out first?

ZELDA (*Very softly*): Good night, Scott.

SCOTT (*Raising his voice*): What's that? You're going to bed now? It's broad daylight. (*More loudly.*) What? "Good night?" (*Suddenly anxious.*) All right, Zelda. Your terms. I agree. I'll get you out. I'm on my way.

> **SCOTT** *hurries left, realizes there is a wall there, hurries right, discovers the receiver in his hand, drops it in the wastebasket, grabs his hat from the coat tree. Exit right.* **ZELDA** *stands motionless. The* **DOCTOR** *enters up left, remains in the lengthening shadows.* **GERALD** *enters left, hesitates, approaches to within ten feet of* **ZELDA**, *stops.*

DOCTOR: There. You see, Zelda? A visitor after all.

GERALD (*Tentatively*): Zelda?

> *No response. Suddenly* **ZELDA** *gasps, turns away from* **GERALD**, *who glances at the* **DOCTOR** *before he speaks again.*

GERALD It's me. Gerald.

ZELDA: It's after hours.

GERALD: Yes, I suppose it is, but the doctor…

ZELDA: The doctor doesn't make the rules. The rules float above her. If she doesn't cling to them, she'll drown.

GERALD *looks at the* DOCTOR,
who makes encouraging gestures.

GERALD (*One step closer*):   How have you been,
Zelda?

ZELDA (*Still averted*): Thank you for visiting me,
Gerald. Did Scott put you up to it?

GERALD (*Another step*): Scott…?

ZELDA (*Turning further away*): Keep your distance.

GERALD: Why, Zelda? What is it?

Slight pause.

ZELDA: My face.

DOCTOR (*Quietly, remaining where she is*): She thinks
she's broken out. She believes it's worst on her face.

ZELDA (*Still averted*): My face is soft and smooth, of
course. (*Drawing the fingers of both hands down her
face.*) I only imagine this bursting, this draining…

GERALD: You're still beautiful, Zelda.

ZELDA (*Her back to* GERALD, *no longer scratching*):
Remember the time Scott threw your finest crystal over
the cliff, Gerald? Reality—or illusion?

GERALD: Reality.

ZELDA: And the time I jumped off the balcony?

GERALD: Reality.

ZELDA: Sara expected to find me on the rocks, didn't
she?

GERALD: Yes.

ZELDA: You see? This is reality. You think it shouldn't
be made visible? You think we have the faces of babes
and angels? For pity's sake, Gerald, open your eyes.
Look!

She faces him suddenly, expecting him to be horrified. Instead he opens his arms.

ZELDA: Are you blind, Gerald? Can't you see?
GERALD: I can see.
ZELDA: Well, if I'm not the monster, who is, Gerald? You?

ZELDA scratches her arms violently.

GERALD: Don't do that, Zelda.
ZELDA: Why not?
GERALD: You're making me itch.

They laugh, come together, arms about each other.

ZELDA: Gerald, do you know who I am?
GERALD: I always thought I did. (*Gently.*) No. Who?
ZELDA: I'll give you a hint: wherever man stands up from an empty desk, there I am.
GERALD (*Protesting*): Zelda…
ZELDA: The dancer is unreconciled. The day is waste. The day before is unredeemed. Think of him, Gerald.
GERALD: Who?
ZELDA: That man. What never left his fingers, Gerald? What never got beyond his wrists?
GERALD: Think of yourself, Zelda. Get better.
ZELDA (Looking at him): Gerald, why don't you worship me?
GERALD: I do. I always have. (*Quietly insistent.*) Get better, Zelda.
ZELDA: Here? Look at the others. (*Quietly.*) Look at HER. (*They glance at the* **DOCTOR**, *stifle a laugh.*) How will I ever get better in this company?

GERALD: Ours wasn't always the best. The best for you.

ZELDA: You're right, Gerald. No more parties. Cancel my invitation.

GERALD (Slanting a line through the air): It's canceled.

ZELDA: Now go.

GERALD: What?

ZELDA: No supplications, Gerald. Time's up.

GERALD: I just got here.

ZELDA: Gerald…

> *Slight pause.*

GERALD: Why?

ZELDA: I don't want you to hear me scream.

> **ZELDA**'s *hands rise to her face. The* **DOCTOR** *is signaling* **GERALD** *to leave. Suddenly he does, the way he came.* **ZELDA**, *apparently under control, loosens her hands. Suddenly she opens her mouth wide, but there is no scream. Instead, she closes it, walks calmly downstage.*

ZELDA (*Not to the audience, not to herself*): Zelda doesn't know the fire is coming, that only a slipper will be left. Zelda is fifteen, posing in her tutu; she's ten, walking on the roof. She has to be careful. To the left is self-destruction, fame. To the right, a terrible propriety, silence.

DOCTOR (*In the same place*): Zelda?

ZELDA (*Not facing her*): Yes, doctor?

DOCTOR (*Holding up a telegram*): Scott's coming.

*Blackout left. In the spill from the
ensuing scene right, ZELDA is just
visible seated on her bench, holding
her slippers in her lap. Right, the desk
is gone; the two chairs, both with
arms, are lined up together near
center. SCOTT, still in Hollywood
suit and tie, occupies the right one;
MONSIGNOR in full ecclesiastical
regalia (purples), the left. He is very
overweight, very pale and wears very
thick glasses. Yet he is as gracious as
GERALD. The low persistent hum of
the engines. SCOTT and
MONSIGNOR are holding onto their
seats. MONSIGNOR looks down to
his left, crosses the fingers on both
hands.*

SCOTT: I thought priests prayed.
MONSIGNOR: I'm saving that for last.

*The plane tosses wildly, as evidenced
by its sound. Both cling to their seats.
When the plane steadies, SCOTT
offers a pint in a paper bag to
MONSIGNOR.*

SCOTT: Perhaps, under the circumstances…
MONSIGNOR: Not at all. Even in the best of times.
(*Swigs, rolls his eyes.*) Good stuff. (*Returns it to
SCOTT, who swigs.)* Well, Scott. (SCOTT chokes.) Oh
yes, I know you. (*Patting him on the back.*) Don't rush
things now. What is it this time: off to boarding school,
hoping to make the team? (SCOTT, *recovering, shakes
his head.*) Princeton maybe? Going to stand for Cottage?

SCOTT (*Getting his breath*): ...no...!

MONSIGNOR: But the yearly musical! Wouldn't miss that for the world. I thought you'd written the book this year.

SCOTT: Not me. Health. Grades. Complicated story.

He swigs, passes bottle.

MONSIGNOR (*Swigs*): I never liked airplanes. (*Returns bottle.*)

SCOTT: I didn't know you flew. (*Swigs.*)

MONSIGNOR: Oh, yes. Whenever possible.

SCOTT (*Swig, gulp*): But didn't you...? I mean in '19? I went to your...

MONSIGNOR: No, no you didn't. Yes, indeed it was. Nineteen. Sweet of you to remember. But what about you, my boy? Keeping up your Aquinas? It's one of those things, isn't it: heading east? I've headed east myself. What is it this time, Scott? Something hopeless?

SCOTT: How did you know?

MONSIGNOR: The shadow about the eyes, my friend. But you're going anyway. That's right. (*The plane lurches. He mumbles.*) Heavenly father, now and in the hour of our...

SCOTT: I, too, have a vision. I'll share it with you.

MONSIGNOR: Why, thank you, Scott.

SCOTT: I see a plane smashing into a mountain.

MONSIGNOR: Thank you very much.

SCOTT: I see the people torn, burnt.

MONSIGNOR: I don't care if I am dead, Scott, these things terrify me.

SCOTT: And my...alter ego...dead among the others.

MONSIGNOR: Amen. Thanks for the vision, Scott. How is Zelda anyway?

SCOTT: But the salient fact, note this...

MONSIGNOR: I'm listening.

SCOTT: Their goods and chattels, their earthly treasures...
MONSIGNOR: Indeed.
SCOTT: Are spread all over the mountain.
MONSIGNOR: I see.
SCOTT: One day...
MONSIGNOR: Perhaps the following year, after the snows melt.
SCOTT: ...some children happen by.
MONSIGNOR: Ah, the children.
SCOTT: They find...a watch, jewelry, my hero's briefcase.
MONSIGNOR: And the bodies.
SCOTT: Yes.
MONSIGNOR: I see: to keep mum and profit, or...
SCOTT: I've seen wealth, you know. I've touched it. This wreck, these trinkets, the dead...are my vision of America.
MONSIGNOR: Is it, Scott? Is it finished? The final version is not the first draft, only shinier, you know. Your vision of greed and innocence and death is only a burlesque, a musical comedy version, of what you might have, given another month or two, another year... How long, Scott?
SCOTT: I don't know.
MONSIGNOR: And how long have you got? (*Slight pause.*) I think I can tell you now: you're flying to a fire that will be put out some eight years after you stop trying.
SCOTT: I'm flying into a mountain.
MONSIGNOR: Put it your own way. Remember, Scott: the smallest changes are the largest. Those last touches... (*Standing.*) Yes. If you'll forgive me now... (*Stepping over* **SCOTT**'*s knees.*) This is where I get off.
SCOTT: I thought we were in a Ford Trimotor.

MONSIGNOR (*In the "aisle"*): You may be. I'm in a Stanley Steamer. Blessings. My best to the Mrs. Sorry I never met her.

> *As* **MONSIGNOR** *proceeds up the "aisle," the roar of the engines changes for the worse. The plane dives.* **SCOTT** *holds onto his seat. The light fades on him, rises on* **ZELDA**, *who suddenly stands and runs right, only to find the* **DOCTOR** *standing in front her.*

DOCTOR (*Gently*): Where are you going?

ZELDA: To my husband.

DOCTOR: Your husband's coming here, Zelda.

ZELDA: Is he?

DOCTOR: You have only to wait for him. Can you do that?

ZELDA: Yes. I don't know.

DOCTOR (*Taking her arm*): Shall we walk down to the gate?

ZELDA (*Starting*): Yes. (*Stopping.*) Doctor?

DOCTOR: What is it?

ZELDA: Is my child…going to be like me?

DOCTOR (*Moving her along*): In what way, Zelda? She's sure to be beautiful, intelligent…

> *As* **ZELDA** *and the* **DOCTOR** *exit left, the rays of the late afternoon sun fade on them.* **SCOTT** *is once more visible, seated in the other chair. His father,* **EDWARD**, *elegant and fragile, occupies the chair at his right.*

SCOTT (*Recognizing him*): Well, I'll be!

EDWARD (*Watching the passing scene, left and right*): How's it going, Scott? We're all proud of you. Your mother…

SCOTT: I'm glad you're here. There's something I've been wanting to say to you.

EDWARD: Where you headed, Scott? How's Zelda?

SCOTT: She's…

EDWARD: Be patient, Scott. These things take time.

SCOTT: I hope you don't think I…

EDWARD: These things…happen, Scott.

SCOTT: I'm glad you understand.

EDWARD: Scott, can you keep a secret?

SCOTT: Why sure, Dad.

EDWARD: I'm in wholesale groceries, you know.

SCOTT: Yes.

EDWARD (*Leaning closer*): My desk is full of dried apricots.

SCOTT: That's the secret?

EDWARD: Sometimes I just…sit there. You've seen me. You thought, as any boy would, I was holding up my end… I just wanted you to know.

SCOTT: Dad, listen, I…

EDWARD (*Standing*): This is my stop, Scott. You know I never liked streetcars. I'll sit at my desk. I'll have an apricot. Good-bye, Scott.

> **EDWARD** *makes his way up the "aisle."*

SCOTT: Dad?

EDWARD (*Stopping at the rear exit*): What is it, Scott?

SCOTT: Any words for me?

> *Slight pause.*

EDWARD: I can't think of any.

SCOTT: That's okay. Don't…
EDWARD: Oh, Scott.
SCOTT: Yes, Dad?
EDWARD: No, nothing.

> *As the light fades,* **EDWARD** *immobile at the rear exit,* **SCOTT** *stands, shouts into the darkness upstage.*

SCOTT: Dad! I understand! I've got a little place downtown: four walls, a desk. No one knows. That's where I bang them out, Dad, the stories.
EDWARD (*No longer visible*): But which stories, Scott? Which stories?

> *Sound of rain in the darkness. The light rises to a very low level. It is a night scene. The stage is opened up, usable in its entirety;* **ZELDA**'s *institution and* **SCOTT**'s *Hollywood office are gone.* **SCOTT** *stands where he stood. RING, disheveled, a fifth in his hand, faces him a few feet away. They are barely visible.*

RING: If it weren't beneath my dignity, buddy, I'd say we were lost.
SCOTT: How can we be lost? I knew where we were just a moment ago.
RING: Okay, smart guy. Where were we?
SCOTT: In the Rolls.
RING: Are we in the Rolls now?
SCOTT: No
RING: Where is the Rolls?
SCOTT: I don't know.

RING: Good thing it was secondhand.
SCOTT: Damn good thing.

> *They share the fifth, separate to look in
> different directions.*

SCOTT (*Looking one way*): Looks like White Bear to me.
RING (*Looking the other*): Never heard of it. This is Great Neck.
SCOTT: The hell it is. I remember!
RING: Yeah.
SCOTT: We stopped to buy gas, remember?
RING: Yeah.
SCOTT: A desolate place: billboards, gas stations…
RING: So you said.
SCOTT: Then we must have wandered off. Simple as that.

> *They come together.*

RING: That simple. Then all we have to do is wander back.
SCOTT: That's it.

> *They share the fifth.*

RING: Were we alone, Scott?
SCOTT: What do you mean?
RING: I seem to remember a woman.
SCOTT: A woman? What sort of woman? (**RING** *makes a coke bottle shape in the air.*) I see (*Worried.*) Ring?
RING: What is it, Scott?
SCOTT: Ring, she must be lost.
RING: So are we, buddy, so are we.

SCOTT: It must be terrible. Her shoes...
RING: What about her shoes?
SCOTT: Think of it, Ring: a woman's shoes, a night like this.
RING: I see what you mean.
SCOTT (*Calling one way*): Woman...!
RING (*Calling the other*): Woman...! Say, isn't this Joseph Conrad's house?
SCOTT: Frankly, I doubt it.
RING (*Sniffing air*): What's that, my boy?
SCOTT (*Sniffing*): Damned if I know.
RING: The sea, Scott, the sea!
SCOTT: You're right! Where is the old so-and-so? (*Raising his voice slightly.*) Joseph? (*Thick Polish accent.*) "He was an inch, perhaps two, under six feet..."

> *They laugh, guzzle, begin to dance a jig, stop, call together.*

BOTH: Joseph!!!
SCOTT: Wouldn't we laugh if the old guy wandered out?

> *Rain ends. Lawn party lights blink on.* **EDWARD** *enters left, walking backwards, pursued by* **SARA**. **SCOTT** *and* **RING**, *more disheveled than ever and, luckily, unseen, keep to the fringes of the party. The guests are suitably attired for the cocktail hour. They carry full glasses.*

SARA: So you're Scott's father! I understand you have Southern blood.
EDWARD: Don't believe everything you hear, Mrs. Murphy.

ZELDA (*Off*): What IS the flapper? What IS the flapper?

SCOTT (*To* **RING**): Zelda always had an ear for the big questions.

> *Enter* **ZELDA** *in party dress, glass in hand.*

SARA: But tell us, Zelda. We want your definition. Don't we, Gerald?

> *Enter* **GERALD**.

GERALD: Of course.

> **SCOTT** *makes a small gesture to* **ZELDA** *from the fringe, but she does not see him.*

EDWARD: Does she vote, Zelda? Excuse me, Mrs. Murphy.

> *Enter* **MONSIGNOR**.

MONSIGNOR: Does she pray?

> *Enter* **SCOTTIE**.

SCOTTIE: Est-ce qu'elle a les enfants?
ZELDA: Please. One at a time.

> **SCOTT** *makes a small gesture to* **SCOTTIE**. **SCOTTIE** *returns it.*

ZELDA: Does she have children? Only if the children are exceptional. Does she vote? Only to break a tie. Does she pray? Only when she's in hell.
MONSIGNOR (*Savoring it*): Ah, hell!

A touch of distant summer thunder to which no one pays any attention.

SARA (*Coaching*): Reality and illusion, Zelda, reality and illusion.
ZELDA: Reality is the exchange rate of the U.S. dollar. Illusion is snakes.
GERALD: Snakes?
ZELDA: Unless I have it backwards.
MONSIGNOR: What does Scott say? By the way, where is Scott?
ZELDA: Scott is in the wine cellar. He'll be here momentarily.
SARA: Do Americans have wine cellars now?
SCOTTIE: Nous n'avons pas même une maison.
ZELDA: Bunny!

Enter **BUNNY***, carrying table full of drinks to which* **RING** *and* **SCOTT***, raising the bottle in the toasts here and there, and only briefly seen by guests who doubt their vision, immediately gravitate.*

BUNNY: Hi, everybody. It's me.
ZELDA: This is Scott's conscience, everyone.
BUNNY: Yes. Where is the old stinker?
SCOTTIE: Il est dans les caves.
ZELDA: Bunny, Mr. Fitzgerald. Mrs. Murphy, Bunny. Oh, but you know Gerald and Sara. My sometime daughter, Scottie. (*For him alone.*) Tell me, Bunny. Do

you notice anything odd about her? Does she seem all right to you?

> **BUNNY** *opens his mouth to speak, but* **ZELDA** *proceeds normally with his introduction.*

ZELDA: And don't let me forget our resident dead priest whom, unfortunately, I never met...
BUNNY: Where's Scott?
ZELDA: I thought he was with you. Monsignor, Bunny.
MONSIGNOR: Bunny, Bunny. Where have I heard that name before?
SCOTTIE: Dans les journeaux, mon père.
MONSIGNOR: That must be it. Are you a cartoonist, Mr. Bunny?
BUNNY: I'm a character.
EDWARD: I want to thank you for your influence on my boy, sir.
BUNNY: Where the hell is Scott?

> *The thunder rumbles closer.*

MONSIGNOR: Careful, Mr. Bunny. Don't play with fire.

> **SCOTTIE** *laughs.*

ZELDA (*Worried, to him alone*): Gerald, Gerald. This is Scott's party.
GERALD: He'll be along. I wonder what's keeping him.
SARA (*To* **ZELDA**): Don't worry, dear.
BUNNY: I know: we'll call him. Come on, everybody. (*Leading a ragged chorus.*) Scott, where the hell?
OTHERS: Where the hell? Where the hell?

Thunder. A brief flash of summer lightning. **SCOTTIE** *produces a telegram.*

SCOTTIE: Poste, téléphone, télégraph!
ZELDA: What is it?
MONSIGNOR: Your child with a telegram, my dear.
ZELDA *(Concerned)*: Bunny, see what it is, will you?

BUNNY takes the telegram, opens it.

SEVERAL: Read it! Read it!
BUNNY *(Reading, making the most out of it)*: Scott Fitzgerald…says the poor…are just like you and me.
MONSIGNOR: Hell, we knew that. Ooops!

Overhead lightning, the stage turned white, an immediate crack of thunder. Blackout. Light as in **SCOTT** *and* **RING** *scene.* **ZELDA** *crawling in her party dress. The rest are gone, except for* **SCOTT** *and* **RING**, *who, having acquired something of the party air, though they remain disheveled, stand properly with glasses in their hands. Sound of rain.* **ZELDA** *neither sees nor hears* **SCOTT**.

SCOTT: Zelda!
ZELDA: Has anyone seen…?
RING: What is it, pretty lady?
ZELDA: …my watch… I had a beautiful watch.
SCOTT: Never mind your watch. Get up before…
ZELDA: Help me, Ring.
RING: How can I…?

ZELDA: Look. Diamond and platinum, "From Scott to Zelda, 1920."

> **RING** *gets slowly down, then* **SCOTT**. *All search on hands and knees.*

RING: How did you…?
ZELDA: I was so foolish. I waved from the train.
SCOTT: You should never wave from the train.
RING (*Searching*): Let's see… "From Scott to Zelda"…"from Scott to Zelda…"
SCOTT (*Searching*): Don't believe her, Ring. I never… It was some trinket Edouard dropped when he buzzed the villa, along with a bottle of Eau de Vie and his bar bill for me to pay.
RING: Here it is!

> **RING**, *still on his knees, holds his closed hand as* **ZELDA**, *still on her knees, kisses him.*

ZELDA: Oh, Ring! It's a miracle. Where is it?
RING: I'm sorry. I thought I…

> **SCOTT** *watches from a distance as* **RING** *opens his empty hand.* **ZELDA**, *in intense pain, turns away, curling into the mud as the light fades. Almost immediately it rises to a very low level.* **RING** *and* **ZELDA** *are gone.* **SCOTT** *is on his knees, barely visible, in the same place. The* **DOCTOR** *stands at some distance from him. Only her white jacket can be seen. The rain has stopped.*

SCOTT: I don't suppose this… Is this the gate?
DOCTOR: I'm sorry, Mr. Fitzgerald. She's not here.
SCOTT: Not here?
DOCTOR: Your wife waited as long as she could.
SCOTT: I've come a long way, doctor.
DOCTOR: I know you have, Mr. Fitzgerald, but there would be no point in making exceptions.
SCOTT: Why not?
DOCTOR: She wouldn't know you.
SCOTT: Wouldn't know…!
DOCTOR: You've been drinking.
SCOTT: I haven't…
DOCTOR: I'm sorry, Mr. Fitzgerald. You're unrecognizable. Why don't you write us next week?
SCOTT: Write!
DOCTOR: That is, if you have time.

As the rain returns and the light fades, **SCOTT** *slowly bows his head.*

Act IV

Since in a few minutes the Hollywood apartment and the hospital bed will be required, this scene can be played in front of the curtain, if there is one, otherwise down right. The light reveals **SCOTT**, *his clothes in order, and still kneeling, though he faces in the other direction. Before him stands a full-size desk and chair. A quarter ream of blank paper rests on the desk, a pen rests on the paper.*

SCOTT (*Standing*): Four walls. A desk! (*Entering that space.*) I don't think I'll even ask how I got here. No.

> **SCOTT** *sits at the desk, runs his hands over the paper, picks up the pen, begins to write.* **ZELDA**'s *voice, soft, intimate, is heard over the loudspeaker.*

VOICE: Scott?
SCOTT (*Writing, softly*): What?
VOICE: This is no time to be writing.
SCOTT: Isn't it? I've got to keep ahead of you, don't I?
VOICE: No, Scott. You don't.

> **SCOTT** *continues writing. There is a tapping sound. He stops, listens, writes again. Once more, the tapping.* **SCOTT**, *stopping, keeps the pen in his hand.*

SCOTT: Damn! Who is it?

> *Enter* **ZELDA** *right. Discreetly, expensively dressed; young, energetic, normal.*

ZELDA: Scott! Thank God I found you.

SCOTT: Who told you about this place?

ZELDA (*Suave, sophisticated*): You did. You were quite conspiratorial about it.

SCOTT: Well, if I did, I did. What do you want?

ZELDA: You'll never guess who's blown into town.

SCOTT: Who?

> **ZELDA** *holds up a note which* **SCOTT** *quickly scans.*

SCOTT: Well, what are they doing here?

ZELDA: They said no trip to America would be complete without a visit to St. Paul.

SCOTT: You can tell they're world travelers.

ZELDA: They're sorry we had such a shitty time in Europe; they hope they'll have a better time here.

SCOTT: That's letting us know.

ZELDA: Anyway, I'm rounding everyone up. And shall we have your father, Bunny, that old priest...?

SCOTT: I suppose.

ZELDA: I've called the caterers. Will you take care of the drinks?

SCOTT: When are they getting here?

ZELDA: Three.

SCOTT: Three! I haven't...

ZELDA (*Leaving right*): Oh, and Scott: could you just meet them at the station?

Exit **ZELDA**. **SCOTT** *looks at his watch, begins slowly to write.* **BUNNY**'s *voice, soft, intimate, is heard over the loudspeaker.*

VOICE: Scott…
SCOTT (*Not looking up, softly*): This is where I bang them out, Bunny.
VOICE: Bang them out, Scott?
SCOTT (*Softly*): The stories, Bunny. No one knows.

BUNNY *bursts in right.*

BUNNY: Scott!
SCOTT (*Writing, not looking up, normally*): I didn't know you were in town.
BUNNY: I'm not. I mean…the whole gang's here. Scott?
SCOTT (*Writing*): What?
BUNNY: We're going to have a party.
SCOTT (*Writing*): So? Where?
BUNNY: At the club. I thought you knew.
SCOTT (*Writing*): Who told you about this place, Bunny?
BUNNY: Everyone knows, Scott.
SCOTT (*Writing*): How does everyone know, Bunny?
BUNNY: Zelda…

SCOTT *stops writing.*

SCOTT: What about Zelda?
BUNNY: Never mind, Scott. We're going to have fun.
SCOTT: That's good. Well, I'd like to, Bunny, but we have a party of our own going. I'm in charge of drinks.
BUNNY (*Another voice*): Naturally.
SCOTT: Pardon?

BUNNY: But Scott, we're relying on you. An entertainment of some sort, an event. Don't let us down.
SCOTT (*Putting down pen*): Well...
BUNNY (*The other voice*): That's the way.
SCOTT: What?
BUNNY: Yes?
SCOTT: I was just thinking...
BUNNY (*The other voice*): Were you?
SCOTT: ...maybe when I get my party going, I can sneak out and make it over to yours.
BUNNY: That's the idea. (**SCOTT** *takes up his pen.*) Or...
SCOTT: Or?
BUNNY: If they don't mind slumming...
SCOTT: You mean drag them along.
BUNNY: We could use an audience.
SCOTT: What about transportation?
BUNNY: Well, let's see. There's your Rolls, of course.
SCOTT: Of course. (*Suddenly.*) We could put the rest in taxis.
BUNNY: That's the idea. (*Looking at his watch.*) Say, we've got some organizing to do.
SCOTT (*Standing*): I'll say we have.

> **BUNNY**, *gesturing "Come on," exits right.* **SCOTT** *looks at the pen in his hand as the light fades.*

> *The light rises once more on a split stage. Right: a Hollywood apartment; armchair, fireplace, books.* **SCOTT**, *in old smoking jacket, sits in the armchair eating a chocolate bar, reading the Princeton alumni paper. Left: the hospital bed, a suggestion of barred windows.* **ZELDA**, *her hair cut*

short, in hospital gown and embroidered slippers, sits on the edge of the bed. She is looking at her feet, listening. **SCOTT** *is also listening. Though they can now hear each other, they do not look at each other until indicated.*

ZELDA: Are you in hell, Scott?
SCOTT: I'm in Hollywood.
ZELDA: I hear…flames.
SCOTT: Do you?
ZELDA (*Looking up*): Are you writing?
SCOTT: I'm thinking. You probably can't see it, but there's a big chart in my mind across which Monroe Stahr pursues Kathleen.
ZELDA: Is she his muse? (*Slight pause.*) You're listening too, aren't you? (*Slight pause.*) To me?
SCOTT: To my heart.

Slight pause.

ZELDA: Hurry and finish, Scott.
SCOTT: There's no hurrying, Zelda. I paid my bills with hurrying.
ZELDA: Maybe just this once… What are you thinking, Scott?
SCOTT: I'm thinking maybe you should get out of there.
ZELDA: I'm not unhappy. There's my novel.

SCOTTIE *appears at* **ZELDA**'s *side. Though she is still nine, she has somehow aged. She always speaks English now; she is sullen and slow to answer.*

ZELDA: Scottie, what are you doing here?
SCOTTIE (*Slight pause*): Visiting.
ZELDA: But you know I'm better. How are you?
SCOTTIE (*Slight pause*): Ungifted. Isn't that strange?
ZELDA: Not so strange, Scottie.
SCOTTIE: But who am I? I'm not you.

> **ZELDA** *looks at her closely.*

SCOTTIE: Am I my father?
ZELDA: You'd better ask him.

> **SCOTTIE**, *unwatched, crosses to*
> **SCOTT** as **ZELDA** *looks down.*

SCOTT: Hello, Scottie. Care for a Hershey's?
SCOTTIE (*Slight pause*): Aren't you even going to ask how I got here?
SCOTT: You're on your own now, Scottie. You can go where you like.
SCOTTIE: I have a question or two.
SCOTT: Shoot.
SCOTTIE: Why do I know so much more than you? Why am I so much stronger? Why...?
SCOTT (*Interrupting*): That's two. Save the rest. Answer them yourself someday.
SCOTTIE: I'm going to do so much more than you.
SCOTT: Good.
SCOTTIE: I won't drink. I won't make a fool of myself. I won't be forgotten in my own lifetime.
SCOTT: Those are the won'ts. What are the wills?
SCOTTIE: I...! (*Suddenly younger, taking his hand.*) Daddy, don't go!
SCOTT: I'm not going anywhere, Scottie. You may not see me, but you'll hear me. I'll be right there in back.

SCOTTIE: Dad... Stay!
SCOTT: Stay where, honey? Hollywood's not the place for me.
SCOTTIE: I don't even know you.
SCOTT: You will.
SCOTTIE: How? Can you tell me that?
SCOTT: I can't tell you everything. Go ask your mother a few questions. Have you visited her lately? She loves you, Scottie.

> **SCOTT** *returns to his candy bar.* **SCOTTIE** *crosses to* **ZELDA**, *stands by her.* **ZELDA** *knows she's there, but does not look up.*

SCOTTIE: Aren't you going to go to him? (*Slight pause.*) I don't know you either.

> **SCOTTIE** *begins to leave.*

ZELDA (*Not looking up*): How are you, Scottie? (*Exit* **SCOTTIE**. **ZELDA***'s voice does not change.*) Have you finished school? Have you got a beau?

> *Slowly* **ZELDA** s*tands, goes to the barred window, looks at the ground several floors below.*

ZELDA: What a firetrap. (*Seeing* **SCOTTIE**, *just raising her hand, calling too softly to be heard.*) Scottie. Scot...

> **ZELDA** *raises her eyes to the night sky.*

SCOTT: What is it, Zelda? Are you smoking?

ZELDA: Just burning a little something in the tub, Scott. My clothes.

SCOTT: Clothes?

ZELDA: The ones I designed for myself. You remember.

SCOTT: I remember. You know, Zelda, maybe it wasn't you keeping me from working; maybe…

> SCOTT *slowly raises his hand to his chest.* ZELDA *stays at the window.*

ZELDA: Hold on, Scott. Hold onto me.

SCOTT: Heartburn? That's what I get for going on the wagon. It doesn't agree with me. (*He stands, pours himself a drink, moves slowly about the room.*) Bunny, if you were here, if you were to say "Scott, old sport…" I hope you're not going to start calling me "old sport." (*Tries again.*) "Scott, old friend, you're not looking so well, your hair…" (*Once more.*) "Scott. If anything should happen to you; before the novel's done, that is; if anyone should ask me to take up the words, the notes, the charts in your head, are there any, uh…?" (*Changing direction of his pacing.*) Sorry, Bunny. It's not that I don't want to help but… You've written a line or two. You know. The last touches reveal what an outsider might think you started with: the whole damn structure of it all. No, Bunny. I haven't any hints for you. No suggestions. Well, perhaps one: sit. No reading now. Sit.

> SCOTT *drains his drink, sits in the arm chair, begins to page through his notes.* ZELDA *still stands at the window. Now the* DOCTOR *stands up center behind her,* ZELDA*'s loose manuscript in her hands.*

DOCTOR: Are you going to stand there all night, Zelda? Your daughter's gone. She's got a child of her own. Scott's dead. (**ZELDA** *turns quickly to face her.*) 1948, Zelda. The war's over. March 10th. Spring is in the air. (*Setting the manuscript on the bed.*) By the way, Zelda, I like your pages. Yes, I'd like to take another look at them in the morning, if I may.
ZELDA: Yes, of…
DOCTOR: Did you have a nice visit? I'm locking up now. It's late. Almost midnight.

> *Exit the* **DOCTOR**, *up center.* **ZELDA** *remains at the window, looking at her room.*

ZELDA: Clank. Or was it clink? I'm not afraid. There was a dance in me. Even a book. (*Suddenly rushing right, stopping.*) Scott!! Scott!! They've locked me in, Scott! (*Sinking to the floor,* barely *audible, realistic.*) I'm going to burn.

> **ZELDA** *remains crumpled on the floor.*

SCOTT (*In the armchair*): Listen! Those are the cars. Smell them? What a place to…! And this year—1940, is it?—nothing settled, nothing known! (*Standing.*) Never mind the unknown. It's the unsaid. (*Pours himself a drink, faces the room.*) Last refuge. Temporary. Brief. Delicate, fragile father, is this what you foretold? (*He drinks.*) Now Monroe dies on his mountaintop and Scott in a suburb of Los Angeles. And neither well. One unwritten, one not written out. Borrowed walls, chair. Shall I tell you? Something more was some of the time within reach.

Enter **MONSIGNOR**. *He moves as*
SCOTT *moves, behind him, and*
neither seen nor heard by him.

MONSIGNOR: Well said, my boy. Worthy of a dead
priest. But tell me: have you made arrangements? Oh, I
know: you'll say you've strayed, your Latin's slipped.
No matter. Sudden death is our specialty.
SCOTT (*Sipping, laughing softly*): I wonder what's in
store.
MONSIGNOR: I'm glad you wonder. Frankly, Scott,
I've had a look ahead. Fear not, my friend: you are
invited. And the party, Scott, is a wing-dinger. Some say
it will never end. Oh yes, Zelda's there, for you had one
soul, you two, though you hardly knew it. Gerald and
Ring and Bunny. All the best people. I may be there
myself.
SCOTT: I can see it now.
MONSIGNOR: Yes, Scott. Picture it. The drinks cart is
never empty. The ashtrays are always full. The laughter
never ceases, for it is good party. The Fitzgeralds, having
so recently arrived, keep it, shall we say, alive. The
servants' eyes are glassy, though they smile. What the
hell: it's three o'clock in the morning. There's just the
slightest trickle of saliva on your host's chin, and more
than one blotch on your tie. And something unspeakable
going on in the bathroom. We won't mention it. Though
maybe you can hear it, Scott, with those excellent ears of
yours, for you are still an observer of the human scene
and though comfortably, might I say eternally, afloat,
you are taking mental notes for a book you will begin in
the morning.

SCOTT *sets his drink over the fireplace, knocks several books to the floor.*

MONSIGNOR (*Close behind* SCOTT): Now, Scott, Three a.m., you know.

SCOTT *rips a book apart, tosses the remains on the floor.*

MONSIGNOR: But what about the one in your head, my boy, the one you're sitting down to tomorrow?
SCOTT (*Discovering his own note fallen from a book*): "Dear friend. Don't forget Dostoyevsky or Dickens." (*Letting go of the note.*) Yes, I certainly hope they received their invitations. Perhaps they can share a taxi.

SCOTT *knocks several more books to the floor, then stoops, dusts them off, begins to restore them all to their places.*

SCOTT (*To the books*): Forgive me. You were finished. You have a right to be here. (*Picking up the torn book, laying it over the fireplace.*) Sorry, Ernest.
MONSIGNOR: You have a good heart, Scott. (SCOTT *laughs.*) But what would you give, I wonder, for a year? For two?

SCOTT *picks up his own manuscript, reads to himself silently.*

SCOTT: Wrong. (*Turning page.*) Wrong. Bits of clay, still with my thumb print. I had to write you down because the right word lies so many words the other side of you and...

MONSIGNOR (*In his ear*): For two years, six months, and…

SCOTT (*Sitting, beginning to correct his manuscript*): …and there is no other way to you.

MONSIGNOR (*Rubbing hands together*): Now. Would you like Zelda there? Scottie? How about a brief affair at the post office as the finished book is taken by the clerk? (*Brief choking sound.*) It's over. Scott Fitzgerald is no more.

SCOTT (*Writing; to himself*): I do not think I have the time; I must proceed as if I did.

MONSIGNOR (*Bending closer*): What the hell, Scott. December 21st, my boy. Let's talk turkey.

SCOTT: "Where youth grows pale…" Sounds familiar. (*Crosses a line out.*)

MONSIGNOR: Damn it, Scott. December 27th, a few friends, Rockville Union Cemetery. Not, I repeat, not the Catholic cemetery where your father lies.

SCOTT (*Not writing, listening to his body*): Zelda?

> **ZELDA**, *still on the floor, lifts her head, but not to look at* **SCOTT**.

ZELDA: Scott? Can I get there if I start now?

MONSIGNOR (*Near center*): Perhaps you can meet halfway. (*To* **SCOTT**.) I'm sorry my position prevents me from dragging you down at the end. (T*o* **ZELDA** *too.*) Until then, you two. Au revoir.

> *Exit* **MONSIGNOR** *up right. There is a faint suggestion of flames beyond the bars, left; the sun comes out just before setting over the Pacific, right. The acting areas are dark enough to be dominated by these lights from the*

wings. **SCOTT** *and* **ZELDA** *do not look at each other.*

SCOTT: The air stinks. The sun is going to show itself once more over a sea I hardly knew was there.
ZELDA: I smell the pear tree, Scott. My window's open. I think the judge has just stepped out on the porch a moment before bed. He sees, in the darkness, a world that he understands.
SCOTT: Oh, the elegance of it! Fragile man, my father. His walk down Summit Avenue. And his code: "these things, Scott, but not these."
ZELDA: The judge says, "Baby? Baby, are you asleep? Just look out the window for a moment, Baby. Look at that!"
SCOTT: "Stand back! Stand back, Scott. Look at it. Take one good look." (*More softly.*) "I walk down Summit Avenue and I'm afraid you'll try so hard not to be like me you might succeed. Stand back!"
ZELDA: What, judge? What are you talking about?
SCOTT: Zelda. I don't think I'm going to get out of this chair.
ZELDA (*Standing, head bowed*): Oh no, judge. It wasn't anything like that. The old woman held a tray of sweets, beautifully arranged. We all stopped to admire. Scott gave a kick. For the extra point, you know. Her little horns of plenty went everywhere. (*Wanting to drop to the floor, to gather.*) I'll pick them up, judge. I'll pick them all up.
SCOTT: Those little horns of plenty offended me. To think that it was all there before us, all the time, that we had only to reach out and... (*Suddenly scribbling a note.*) " Do not forget Flaubert or James." (*Inserting it in a book; looking up, but not at* **ZELDA**.) Zelda, does your heart ever stop? Oh, just for a second.

ZELDA: Is your floor warm? If you put your ear to the floor, Scott, do you hear screams?

> *The* **DOCTOR** *appears behind* **ZELDA,** *barely visible in the shadows. She speaks in the voice of* **ZELDA***'s mother.*

DOCTOR: "I woke up hot, child. I thought you were having a nightmare. I went to your room. The window was open. The moonlight fell across the bed. You were gone, of course. Grown up, married. I was so tired. I leaned on the windowsill. I smelled the pear."

ZELDA: Scott, I'm afraid.

DOCTOR (*As before*): "I thought: Judge, I never knew her; did you? Then I remembered. The judge was gone too."

SCOTT: Oh, oh. (*Holding his hand level before him.*) I think I've got the jitters, Zelda. Noncombatant shell shock, you know.

DOCTOR: He's at Verdun, Zelda. He's peering through the grate. "All those unidentified," he says. "Mark it down."

ZELDA (*Indirectly*): Scott...

SCOTT: Too much coffee, Zelda. Too much hanging around the commissary gawking at the stars. Did I ever tell you I was the invisible man? Yes, sir. Step right up! See the man who isn't there. When they said "Here comes Scott Fitzgerald," I wasn't even born. They opened doors for the apprentice boy. They close them in front of the man who got three lines right this morning, who will get three right this afternoon!

DOCTOR (*Mother's voice*): "I've sat down on your old bed. I've fallen asleep. I'm alone in the house now. I can't get used to it. I dream...there's something wrong somewhere, that newfangled wiring. I dream...there's fire. I dream I'm waking you up, Baby. Wake up, Baby! Get out of here!"

SCOTT (*Sudden pain*): Ah! A hand pulling me down. Where is that fellow?

ZELDA (*Not looking*): Scott. Pick up the telephone. Call.

DOCTOR (*Mother's voice*): "Then the dream passes. I'm alone again, in your room. Won't you visit, Ba…?"

ZELDA: Are you smoking, Scott?

SCOTT (*Sudden pain*): Ah! Monsignor! For the completion of one short novel…herein referred to by its working title…I…

DOCTOR (*Mother's voice*): "Is he at his typewriter, Baby? Is he praying?"

ZELDA: Scott!

DOCTOR (*As before, leaving*): "I'm going back to my room, Baby. The sheets must be cool."

Exit **DOCTOR**.

SCOTT (*Out of pain*): Well. There. It's past.

> **ZELDA** *senses her mother's presence at the moment she becomes aware of the* **DOCTOR**'*s departure.*

ZELDA: Mother?

> **ZELDA** *turns to look at nothing. Suddenly she rushes to where the* **DOCTOR** *vanished, stops; then rushes to the window, stops.*

ZELDA: Mother?

SCOTT (*To himself*): I was always embarrassed by my mother. She had some very odd habits. She died.

ZELDA *rests her head against the bars. A faint light flickers on her skin.*

SCOTT (*Not looking, to himself*): I wonder: do we cry when there's no one left to cry for us, or when there's no one left to cry for? (*Looking at the manuscript in his lap.*) What's this? A parody, a minstrel show? My black man on the beach won't do for my views on art. Yes, I see it now.

> *Having crossed out, he begins to write. Suddenly, silently, he stands straight, clutching his chest, falls full-length. His loose manuscript scatters around him. His light fades.* **ZELDA** *goes quickly to her bed, sits clutching her manuscript to her breast, her mind on* **SCOTT**. *Light rises right on* **SCOTT** *lying at* **RING**'s *feet. Armchair, fireplace, and books are gone. A half-light which is not enough to disturb the relative darkness where* **ZELDA** *remains visible and motionless.* **RING** *is formally dressed.* **SCOTT** *looks at his shining black shoes.*

SCOTT: Say, old buddy, where's that party of ours?
RING: Party's over, Scott. We had a hell of a time.
SCOTT (*Shaking head*): We did?
RING: Zelda sang and you danced.
SCOTT: I...
RING: You danced and Zelda sang.
SCOTT (*Sitting up*): And my novel?
RING: Novel? (*Finding a lady's diamond wrist watch behind* **SCOTT**'s *ear.*) Say, what have we here?

(*Reading the inscription.*) "From Scott to Zelda, 1920."
What do you think of that?
SCOTT (*Standing*): I don't know what to think.
RING: I know. We've got to give it back.
SCOTT: How?
RING: We'll just go back to the party and look for the beauty that's covered with mud.
SCOTT: Wait a minute. You said the party was over.

> *Band, off right, plays "Yes We Have No Bananas."*

RING: I was wrong.

> *Enter* **BUNNY** *right. Black tie. Tray of full champagne glasses. He serves* **RING** *first, who, with his glass in one hand and the watch in the other, waits, looking in the direction of the music.*

BUNNY (*Softly*): Mr. Lardner. (*Serving* **SCOTT**, *normally*.) One for the road, Mr. Fitzgerald?
SCOTT (*Taking a glass*): I'm not going anywhere.
BUNNY: That's what you think.

> **MONSIGNOR** *enters right, robes raised as he hurries to the champagne.* **BUNNY** *moves to serve him, then* **EDWARD,** *who, also formally attired, stands back from the others, right.*

BUNNY (*Softly*): Monsignor. Mr. Fitzgerald.
MONSIGNOR (*Glass in hand, approaching* **SCOTT**): How are you, Scott? Done with flying into mountains?
SCOTT: All done.

MONSIGNOR (*For him alone*): Confidentially, my boy, the party's sagging. We need new blood.
SCOTT: My novel...
MONSIGNOR: Never mind your novel. Where's Sarah Bernhard?

Enter **GERALD**, *black tie, right.*

GERALD: Where is everyone?
BUNNY (*Serving him, softly*): Mr. Murphy.
GERALD: Scott, have you seen Zelda?
SCOTT: Zelda who?

EDWARD*, raising his voice just sufficiently, calls from his position, right.*

EDWARD: Oh, Scott.
SCOTT (*Staying put*): What is it, Dad?
EDWARD (*Lower, but insistent*): Scott.
SCOTT: Yes?

SCOTT finishes his drink. **BUNNY** appears at his side.

BUNNY: Making the hours vanish, sir? You're the magician.
SCOTT (*His mind elsewhere*): What's that? Yes, Bunny, I'm the magician.

SCOTT *takes a full glass.*

BUNNY: An afternoon, an evening. It's the long night, sir. Think you'll sleep through this one?

SCOTT (*As before*): What's that? No, Bunny. I'm wide awake. (*Turning to* **MONSIGNOR**.) Have you noticed? There are no women.
MONSIGNOR (*Taking another glass*): No women. What next? Here's dirt in your eyes, soldier.

> **SCOTT** and **MONSIGNOR** *raise their glasses to each other.* **RING**, *having given up on looking right, returns to* **SCOTT**.

RING: Scott, this party stinks.
MONSIGNOR: Now…
RING (*To* **SCOTT**): I've had enough. Where's the Rolls?
SCOTT: I'm not sure. I didn't… Didn't you…?
MONSIGNOR (*Offering* **SCOTT** *the ground at his feet*): Perhaps you'd like to lie down awhile, Scott, think things over, get them straight…
SCOTT: No! (*Taking the watch from* **RING**.) Give me that. (*Loudly.*) Please. Everyone!

> *The music stops. All look at* **SCOTT**.

SCOTT (*Calmly*): Gentlemen. My friends. It's late. Tomorrow…

> *Light fades right, flames rise off left.* **ZELDA** *stands, dropping the loose pages of her manuscript, and staggers downstage, mouth open. Even as she moves the flames cease.* **SCOTT** *stands right center, alone.* **SCOTT** *and* **ZELDA** *speak normally; they do not face each other. Very dim light.*

ZELDA: What was it like? Did it hurt?

SCOTT: Relatively painless. It was over in a second. And you?

ZELDA: There were some uncomfortable moments.

SCOTT: The smoke?

ZELDA: Yes.

SCOTT: No, I wouldn't care for it.

ZELDA: And what I saw. The others. God help them.

SCOTT: God help them. Still, they were off their rockers.

ZELDA: Not at the end.

SCOTT: The fire cured them. Now why didn't we think of that?

ZELDA: Too simple.

SCOTT: And so. My father's gone. My mother.

ZELDA: My father.

SCOTT: That's about it, isn't it?

ZELDA: What about us?

They face each other. Pause.

SCOTT: I can't bear to think of you that way.

ZELDA (*Staying put, almost silently comforting*): …Scott, Scott…

SCOTT (*In control of himself*): My life, gone, is easier to bear than yours.

ZELDA: Yes.

SCOTT: By the way, your watch… (*Searching his pockets.*) What's wrong with me? Bunny could do it.

ZELDA: Better leave it to him. (*More lightly.*) Some things, Scott…

SCOTT (*Searching*): I know. I know.

> **SCOTT** *turns toward the light to*
> *better search his pockets.* **ZELDA** *sits*

*on the floor; then lies on her back, feet
downstage.*

SCOTT (*Turning*): Here it is! (*He sees.*) Well. (*He
pockets the watch, enters her space.*) Well.

> **SCOTT** *straightens his tie, lies on his
> back beside her.*
>
> *Sound of rain as the light fades, and
> continuing in the darkness.*

www.ingramcontent.com/pod-product-compliance
Lightning Source LLC
Chambersburg PA
CBHW031602040426
42452CB00006B/386